JAMESTOWN 🚢 EDUC

TIMED READINGS

25 Two-Part Lessons
with Questions for
Building Reading Speed and Comprehension

BOOK NINE

Edward Spargo

Glencoe
McGraw-Hill

New York, New York   Columbus, Ohio   Chicago, Illinois   Peoria, Illinois   Woodland Hills, Califorina

JAMESTOWN EDUCATION

Glencoe/McGraw-Hill
A Division of The McGraw·Hill Companies

Timed Readings Plus, Book Nine, Level L
Selection text adapted from Compton's Encyclopedia.
Used with permission of Compton's Learning Company.

ISBN : 0-89061-911-5

Manufactured in the United States of America

Send all Inquiries to:
Glencoe/McGraw-Hill
8787 Orion Place
Columbus, OH 43240-4027

04 05 06 07 08 09 10   045   10 09 08 07 06 05 04 03 02

CONTENTS

To the Instructor

Overview

Timed Readings Plus is designed to develop both reading speed and comprehension. A timed selection in each lesson focuses on improving reading rate. A nontimed selection—the "plus" selection—follows the timed selection. The nontimed selection concentrates on building mastery in critical areas of comprehension.

The 10 books in the series span reading levels 4–13, with one book at each level. Readability of the selections was assessed by using the Fry Readability Scale. Each book contains 25 lessons; each lesson is divided into Parts A and B.

Part A includes the timed selection followed by 10 multiple-choice questions: 5 fact questions and 5 thought questions. The timed selection is 400 words long and contains subject matter that is factual, nonfiction, and textbook-like. Because everyone—regardless of level—reads a 400-word passage, the steps for the timed selection can be concurrent for everyone.

Part B includes the nontimed selection, which is more narrative than the timed selection. The length of the selection varies depending on the subject matter, which relates to the content of the timed selection. The nontimed selection is followed by five comprehension questions that address the following major comprehension skills: recognizing words in context, distinguishing fact from opinion, keeping events in order, making correct inferences, and understanding main ideas.

Getting Started

Begin by assigning students to a level. A student should start with a book that is one level below his or her current reading level. If a student's reading level is not known, a suitable starting point would be one or two levels below the student's present grade in school.

Teaching a Lesson: Part A

Work in each lesson begins with the timed selection in Part A. If you wish to have all the students in the class read a selection at the same time, you can coordinate the timing using the following method. Give students the signal to preview. Allow 15 seconds for this. Have students begin reading the selection at the same time. After one minute has passed, write on the chalkboard the time that has elapsed. Update the time at 10-second intervals (1:00, 1:10, 1:20, etc.). Tell students to copy down the last time shown on the chalkboard when they finish reading. They should then record this reading time in the space designated after the selection.

If students keep track of their own reading times, have them write the times at which they start and finish reading on a separate piece of paper and then figure and record their reading time as above.

Students should now answer the ten questions that follow the Part A selection. Responses are recorded by putting an X in the box next to the student's choice of answer. Correct responses to eight or more questions indicates satisfactory comprehension and recall.

Teaching a Lesson: Part B

When students have finished Part A, they can move on to read the Part B selection. Although brief, these selections deliver all the content needed to attack the range of comprehension questions that follow.

Students next answer the comprehension questions that follow the Part B selection. Directions for answering the questions are provided with each question. Correct responses require deliberation and discrimination.

Correcting and Scoring Answers

Using the Answer Key at the back of the book, students self-score their responses to the questions in Parts A and B. Incorrect answers should be circled and the correct answers should be marked. The number of correct answers for Part A and for Part B and the total correct answers should be tallied on the final page of the lesson.

Using the Graphs

Reading times are plotted on the Reading Rate graph at the back of the book. The legend on the graph automatically converts reading times to words-per-minute rates. Comprehension totals are plotted on the Comprehension Scores graph. Plotting automatically converts the raw scores to a comprehension percentage based on four points per correct answer.

Diagnosis and Evaluation

The Comprehension Skills Profile graph at the back of the book tracks student responses to the Part B comprehension questions. For each incorrect response, students should mark an X in the corresponding box on the graph. A column of Xs rising above other columns indicates a specific comprehension weakness. Using the profile, you can assess trends in student performance and suggest remedial work if necessary.

A student who has reached a peak in reading speed (with satisfactory comprehension) is ready to advance to the next book in the series. Before moving on to the next book, students should be encouraged to maintain their speed and comprehension on a number of lessons in order to consolidate their achievement.

How to Use This Book

Getting Started

Study Part A: Reading Faster and Better. Read and learn the steps to follow and the techniques to use to help you read more quickly and more efficiently.

Study Part B: Mastering Reading Comprehension. Learn what the five categories of comprehension are all about. Knowing what kind of comprehension response is expected from you and how to achieve that response will help you better comprehend all you read.

Working a Lesson

Find the Starting Lesson. Locate the timed selection in Part A of the lesson that you are going to read. Wait for your instructor's signal to preview the selection. Your instructor will allow you 15 seconds for previewing.

Read the Part A Selection. When your instructor gives you the signal, begin reading. Read at a faster-than-normal speed. Read carefully so that you will be able to answer questions about what you have read.

Record Your Reading Time. When you finish reading, look at the blackboard and note your reading time. Write this time at the bottom of the page on the line labeled Reading Time.

Answer the Part A Questions. Answer the 10 questions that follow the selection. There are 5 fact questions and 5 thought questions. Choose the best answer to each question and put an X in that box.

Read the Part B Selection. This passage is less textbook-like and more story-like than the timed selection. Read well enough so that you can answer the questions that follow.

Answer the Part B Questions. These questions are different from traditional multiple-choice questions. In answering these questions, you must make three choices for each question. Instructions for answering each category of question are given. There are 15 responses for you to record.

Correct Your Answers. Use the Answer Key at the back of the book. For the Part A questions, circle any wrong answer and put an X in the box you should have marked. For the Part B questions, circle any wrong answer and write the correct letter or number next to it.

Scoring Your Work

Total Your Correct Answers. Count your correct answers for Part A and for Part B. Record those numbers on the appropriate lines at the end of the lesson. Then add the two scores to determine your total correct answers. Record that number on the appropriate line.

Plotting Your Progress

Plot Your Reading Time. Refer to the Reading Rate graph on page 116. On the vertical line that represents your lesson, put an X at the point where it intersects your reading time, shown along the left-hand side. The right-hand side of the graph will reveal your words-per-minute reading speed. Your instructor will review this graph from time to time to evaluate your progress.

Plot Your Comprehension Scores. Record your comprehension scores on the graph on page 117. On the vertical line that represents your lesson, put an X at the point where it intersects your total correct answers, shown along the left-hand side. The right-hand side of the graph will reveal your comprehension percentage. Your instructor will want to review this graph, too. Your achievement, as shown on both graphs, will determine your readiness to move on to higher and more challenging levels.

Plot Your Comprehension Skills. You will find the Comprehension Skills Profile on page 118. It is used to record your wrong answers only for the Part B questions. The five categories of questions are listed along the bottom. There are five columns of boxes, one column for each question. For every wrong answer, put an X in a box for that question. Your instructor will use this graph to detect any comprehension problems you may be experiencing.

PART A: READING FASTER AND BETTER

Step 1: Preview

When you read, do you start in with the first word, or do you look over the whole selection for a moment? Good readers preview the selection first. This helps make them good—and fast—readers. Here are the steps to follow when previewing the timed selection in Part A of each unit.

1. Read the Title. Titles are designed not only to announce the subject, but also to make the reader think. What can you learn from the title? What thoughts does it bring to mind? What do you already know about this subject?

2. Read the First Sentence. Read the first two sentences if they are short. The opening sentence is the writer's opportunity to greet the reader. Some writers announce what they hope to tell you in the selection. Some writers tell you why they are writing. Other writers just try to get your attention.

3. Read the Last Sentence. Read the final two sentences if they are short. The closing sentence is the writer's last chance to talk to you. Some writers repeat the main idea once more. Some writers draw a conclusion—this is what they have been leading up to. Other writers summarize their thoughts; they tie all the facts together.

4. Scan the Selection. Glance through the selection quickly to see what else you can pick up. Look for anything that can help you read the selection. Are there names, dates, or numbers? If so, you may have to read more slowly. Is the selection informative—containing a lot of facts, or is it conversational—an informal discussion with the reader?

Step 2: Read for Meaning

When you read, do you just see words? Are you so occupied reading words that you sometimes fail to get the meaning? Good readers see beyond the words—they seek the meaning. This makes them faster readers.

1. Build Concentration. You cannot read with understanding if you are not concentrating. When you discover that your thoughts are straying, correct the situation right away. Avoid distractions and distracting situations. Keep the preview information in mind. This will help focus your attention on the selection.

2. Read in Thought Groups. A reader should strive to see words in meaningful combinations. If you see only a word at a time (called word-by-word reading), your comprehension suffers along with your speed.

3. Question the Writer. To sustain the pace you have set for yourself, and to maintain a high level of concentration and comprehension, question the writer as you read. Ask yourself such questions as, "What does this mean? How can I use this information?"

Step 3: Grasp Paragraph Sense

The paragraph is the basic unit of meaning. If you can discover quickly and understand the main point of each paragraph, you can comprehend the writer's message. Good readers know how to find the main ideas quickly. This helps make them faster readers.

1. Find the Topic Sentence. The topic sentence, which contains the main idea, is often the first sentence of a paragraph. It is followed by sentences that support, develop, or explain the main idea. Sometimes a topic sentence comes at the end of a paragraph. When it does, the supporting details come first, building the base for the topic sentence. Some paragraphs do not have a topic sentence; all of the sentences combine to create a meaningful idea.

2. Understand Paragraph Structure. Every well-written paragraph has a purpose. The purpose may be to inform, define, explain, illustrate, and so on. The purpose should always relate to the main idea and expand on it. As you read each paragraph, see how the body of the paragraph is used to tell you more about the main idea.

Step 4: Organize Facts

When you read, do you tend to see a lot of facts without any apparent connection or relationship? Understanding how the facts all fit together to deliver the writer's message is, after all, the reason for reading. Good readers organize facts as they read. This helps them read rapidly and well.

1. Discover the Writer's Plan. Every writer has a plan or outline to follow. If you can discover the writer's method of organization, you have a key to understanding the message. Sometimes the writer gives you obvious signals. The statement, "There are three reasons . . .," should prompt you to look for a listing of the three items. Other less obvious signal words such as *moreover, otherwise,* and *consequently* tell you the direction the writer is taking in delivering a message.

2. Relate as You Read. As you read the selection, keep the information learned during the preview in mind. See how the writer is attempting to piece together a meaningful message. As you discover the relationship among the ideas, the message comes through quickly and clearly.

PART B: MASTERING READING COMPREHENSION

Recognizing Words in Context

Always check to see if the words around a new word—its context—can give you some clue to its meaning. A word generally appears in a context related to its meaning. If the words *soil* and *seeds* appear in an article about gardens, for example, you can assume they are related to the topic of gardens.

Suppose you are unsure of the meaning of the word *expired* in the following paragraph:

> Vera wanted to take a book out, but her library card had expired.
> She had to borrow mine because she didn't have time to renew hers.

You could begin to figure out the meaning of *expired* by asking yourself, "What could have happened to Vera's library card that would make her have to borrow someone else's card?" You might realize that if she had to renew her card, it must have come to an end or run out. This would lead you to conclude that the word *expired* must mean to come to an end or run out. You would be right. The context suggested the meaning to you.

Context can also affect the meaning of a word you know. The word *key*, for instance, has many meanings. There are musical keys, door keys, and keys to solving a mystery. The context in which *key* occurs will tell you which meaning is right.

Sometimes a hard word will be explained by the words that immediately follow it. The word *grave* in the following sentence might give you trouble:

> He looked grave; there wasn't a trace of a smile on his lips.

You can figure out that the second part of the sentence explains the word *grave*: "wasn't a trace of a smile" indicates a serious look, so *grave* must mean serious.

The subject of a sentence and your knowledge about that subject might also help you determine the meaning of an unknown word. Try to decide the meaning of the word *revive* in the following sentence:

> Sunshine and water will revive those drooping plants.

The sentence is about giving plants light and water. You may know that plants need light and water to be healthy. If you know that drooping plants are not healthy, you can figure out that *revive* means to bring back to health.

Distinguishing Fact from Opinion

Every day you are called upon to sort out fact and opinion. When a friend says she saw Mel Gibson's greatest movie last night, she is giving you her opinion. When she says she saw Mel Gibson's latest movie, she may be stating a fact. The fact can be proved—you can check to confirm or verify that the movie is indeed Mel Gibson's most recent film. The opinion can be disputed—ask around and others may not agree about the film's unqualified greatness. Because much of what you read and hear contains both facts and opinions, you need to be able to tell them apart. You need the skill of distinguishing fact from opinion.

Facts are statements that can be proved true. The proof must be objective and verifiable. You must be able to check for yourself to confirm a fact.

Look at the following facts. Notice that they can be checked for accuracy and confirmed. Suggested sources for verification appear in parentheses.

- In 1998 Bill Clinton was president of the United States. (Consult newspapers, news broadcasts, election results, etc.)

- Earth revolves around the sun. (Look it up in encyclopedias or astrological journals; ask knowledgeable people.)

- Dogs walk on four legs. (See for yourself.)

Opinions are statements that cannot be proved true. There is no objective evidence you can consult to check the truthfulness of an opinion. Unlike facts, opinions express personal beliefs or judgments. Opinions reveal how someone feels about a subject, not the facts about that subject. You might agree or disagree with someone's opinion, but you cannot prove it right or wrong.

Look at the following opinions. Reasons for classification as opinions appear in parentheses.

- Bill Clinton was born to be a president. (You cannot prove this by referring to birth records. There is no evidence to support this belief.)

- Intelligent life exists on other planets in our solar system. (There is no proof of this. It may be proved true some day, but for now it is just an educated guess—not a fact.)

- Dog is man's best friend. (This is not a fact; your best friend might not be a dog.)

As you read, be aware that facts and opinions are frequently mixed together. The following passage contains both facts and opinions:

> The new 2000 Cruising Yacht offers lots of real-life interior room. It features a luxurious aft cabin, not some dim "cave." The galley

comes equipped with a full-size refrigerator and freezer. And this spacious galley has room to spare. The heads (there are two) have separate showers. The fit and finish are beyond equal and the performance is responsive and outstanding.

Did you detect that the third and fifth sentences state facts and that the rest of the sentences express opinions? Both facts and opinions are useful to you as a reader. But to evaluate what you read and to read intelligently, you need to know the difference between them.

Keeping Events in Order

Writers organize details in a pattern. They present information in a certain order. Recognizing how writers organize—and understanding that organization—can help you improve your comprehension.

When details are arranged in the precise order in which they occurred, a writer is using a chronological (or time) pattern. A writer may, however, change this order. The story may "flash back" to past events that affected the present. The story may "flash forward" to show the results of present events. The writer may move back and forth between past, present, and future to help you see the importance of events.

Making Correct Inferences

Much of what you read suggests more than it says. Writers do not always state outright what they want you to know. Frequently, they omit information that underlies the statements they make. They may assume that you already know it. They may want you to make the effort to figure out the implied information. To get the most out of what you read, you must come to an understanding about unstated information. You can do this through inference. From what is stated, you make inferences about what is not.

You make many inferences every day. Imagine, for example, that you are visiting a friend's house for the first time. You see a bag of dog food. You infer (make an inference) that the family has a dog. On another day you overhear a conversation. You catch the names of two actors and the words *scene, dialogue,* and *directing.* You infer that the people are discussing a movie or play.

In these situations and others like them, you infer unstated information from what you observe or read. Readers who cannot make inferences cannot see beyond the obvious. For the careful reader, facts are just the beginning. Facts stimulate your mind to think beyond them—to make an inference about what is meant but not stated.

The following passage is about Charles Dickens. As you read it, see how many inferences you can make.

Charles Dickens visited the United States in 1867. Wherever he went, the reception was the same. The night before, crowds arrived and lined up before the door. By morning the streets were campgrounds, with men, women, and children sitting or sleeping on blankets. Hustlers got ten times the price of a ticket. Once inside, audiences were surprised to hear their favorite Dickens characters speak with an English accent. After 76 readings Dickens boarded a ship for England. When his fellow passengers asked him to read, he said he'd rather be put in irons!

Did you notice that many inferences may be drawn from the passage? Dickens attracted huge crowds. From that fact you can infer that he was popular. His English accent surprised audiences. You can infer that many people didn't know he was English. Hustlers got high prices for tickets. This suggests that "scalping" tickets is not new. Dickens refused to read on the ship. You can infer that he was exhausted and tired of reading aloud to audiences. Those are some obvious inferences that can be made from the passage. More subtle ones can also be made; however, if you see the obvious ones, you understand how inferences are made.

Be careful about the inferences you make. One set of facts may suggest several inferences. Not all of them will be correct; some will be faulty inferences. The correct inference is supported by enough evidence to make it more likely than other inferences.

Understanding Main Ideas

The main idea tells who or what is the subject of the paragraph or passage. The main idea is the most important idea, the idea that provides purpose and direction. The rest of the paragraph or passage explains, develops, or supports the main idea. Without a main idea, there would be only a collection of unconnected thoughts. It would be like a handle and a bowl without the "idea cup," or bread and meat without the "idea sandwich."

In the following passage, the main idea is printed in italics. As you read, observe how the other sentences develop or explain the main idea.

> *Typhoon Chris hit with full fury today on the central coast of Japan.* Heavy rain from the storm flooded the area. High waves carried many homes into the sea. People now fear that the heavy rains will cause mudslides in the central part of the country. The number of people killed by the storm may climb past the 200 mark by Saturday.

In this paragraph, the main idea statement appears first. It is followed by sentences that explain, support, or give details. Sometimes the main idea appears at the end of a paragraph. Writers often construct that type of paragraph when their purpose is to persuade or convince. Readers may be more open to a new idea if the reasons for it are presented first. As you read the following paragraph, think about the overall impact of the supporting ideas. Their purpose is to convince the reader that the main idea in the last sentence should be accepted.

> Last week there was a head-on collision at Huntington and Canton streets. Just a month ago a pedestrian was struck there. Fortunately, she was only slightly injured. In the past year there have been more accidents there than at any other corner in the city. In fact, nearly 10 percent of all city accidents occur there. This intersection is dangerous, and a traffic signal should be installed there before a life is lost.

The details in the paragraph progress from least important to most important. They achieve their full effect in the main idea statement at the end.

In many cases, the main idea is not expressed in a single sentence. The reader is called upon to interpret all of the ideas expressed and decide upon a main idea. Read the following paragraph:

> The American author Jack London was once a pupil at the Cole Grammar School in Oakland, California. Each morning the class sang a song. When the teacher noticed that Jack wouldn't sing, she sent him to the principal. He returned to class with a note. It said that he could be excused from singing if he would write an essay every morning.

In this paragraph, the reader has to interpret the individual ideas and decide on a main idea. This main idea seems reasonable: Jack London's career as a writer began with a "punishment" in grammar school.

Understanding the concept of the main idea and knowing how to find it is important. Transferring that understanding to your reading and study is also important.

Pass the Cheese, Please

Long ago, people learned to turn perishable milk into a solid food that would not spoil. Perhaps a nomadic herder discovered cheese when using the stomach of a newly killed calf or young sheep as a milk canteen. Milk-curdling enzymes, essential for cheese making, would have caused the milk in the canteen to separate into a thin greenish-yellow liquid called whey and solids called curds.

All over the world today, the milk of cows, goats, sheep, reindeer, buffaloes, and even horses is used to make cheese. Most cheeses made in the United States and Canada have European origins; and the most popular cheese made in the United States is cheddar, an English cheese, that is often called American cheddar or simply American. Variations in the methods and recipes used to make cheese result in the many different kinds. The amount of water and fat determines whether a cheese will be hard or soft, and the flavor and texture depend largely on the kinds of bacteria that are active in the ripening process.

Natural cheese continues to ripen after it has reached its prime; it also dries out. Processed cheese, with its uniform flavor and texture, lasts longer than natural cheese because processed cheese is pasteurized. A single variety, such as cheddar or Swiss, may be processed, or different types may be blended. Pasteurized cheeses are shredded, mixed with water and salts, and blended at pasteurizing temperature. While still fluid, the mixture is poured into containers. Cheese to be sold in slices is run through rollers and stacked, cut, and packaged. Made soft for spreading, both cheese foods and spreads contain milk solids and sometimes added ingredients, such as relishes, fruits, vegetables, and meat. Spreads have a higher moisture content.

Cheddar, which is a hard, all-purpose cheese that varies in flavor from sharp to mild, comes in different shapes and sizes. Semisoft cheeses slice more easily and are used in sandwiches, on crackers, and as snacks. Dessert cheeses come in small sizes because they are surface ripened. Extremely hard, sharp-flavored cheeses that are low in moisture and milk fat are a specialty of the Italians. Parmesan cheese, for example, is used chiefly in grated form for seasoning soups, spaghetti, and other cooked dishes.

Nutritionists consider cheese one of the best protein foods, but cheese also contains calcium, phosphorus, and essential amino acids. The whole-milk cheeses contain the fat-soluble vitamin A and carotene.

Reading Time _____

Recalling Facts

1. Essential ingredients for making cheese from milk are
   - ❏ a. enzymes.
   - ❏ b. curds.
   - ❏ c. whey.

2. The most popular cheese made in the United States is
   - ❏ a. Swiss.
   - ❏ b. cheddar.
   - ❏ c. parmesan.

3. The hardness of cheese depends on
   - ❏ a. how long it ripens.
   - ❏ b. the kind of animal that produces the milk.
   - ❏ c. the amount of water and fat.

4. The kinds of bacteria that are active in the ripening process determine
   - ❏ a. color.
   - ❏ b. flavor and texture.
   - ❏ c. fat content.

5. After it has reached its prime, natural cheese
   - ❏ a. continues to ripen.
   - ❏ b. stops ripening.
   - ❏ c. absorbs moisture.

Understanding Ideas

6. You can conclude from the article that natural cheese
   - ❏ a. tastes better than processed cheese.
   - ❏ b. keeps longer than processed cheese.
   - ❏ c. is not pasteurized as processed cheese is.

7. It is likely that cheddar cheese is popular because it
   - ❏ a. is an English cheese.
   - ❏ b. comes in a variety of flavors.
   - ❏ c. contains calcium.

8. The more moisture a cheese contains, the
   - ❏ a. more flavorful it is.
   - ❏ b. harder it is.
   - ❏ c. more spreadable it is.

9. Pasteurization is a process that
   - ❏ a. blends different cheeses together.
   - ❏ b. slows spoilage.
   - ❏ c. increases bacteria content.

10. You can conclude that cheese is popular
    - ❏ a. primarily in the United States.
    - ❏ b. primarily in England.
    - ❏ c. around the world.

Do-It-Yourself Cheese

Cheese, a food from ancient times, is made by separating milk curds, or solids, from the whey, or liquid. At one time, all cheeses were made by hand, but now, almost all cheese is mass-produced in factories.

You can get an idea of how cheese is made by using simple ingredients to make yogurt cheese in your own kitchen. Start by making the yogurt. The ingredients are milk and either yogurt starter or plain yogurt that is labeled natural and contains yogurt cultures, the advantageous bacteria that cause milk to form solids. In earlier days, people got their "starters" from friends or family when they set up housekeeping, but you can buy yours in a supermarket.

Heat a quart of milk until it is hot but not boiling, remove it from the heat, and stir in three tablespoons of plain yogurt. Put the mixture in a jar and keep it in a warm place for several hours or overnight. It will form yogurt.

Next, line a strainer or sieve with cheesecloth or a layer of paper towels and place it over a large bowl. Pour in the yogurt and let it drain—at least three hours, but preferably overnight. In the morning, you will have a mild-flavored white cheese inside the strainer. You can add spices or herbs to your cheese and use it as a spread, or you can eat it as is.

1. Recognizing Words in Context

Find the word *advantageous* in the passage. One definition below is a *synonym* for that word; it means the same or almost the same. One definition is an *antonym;* it has the opposite or nearly opposite meaning. The other has a completely different meaning. Label the definitions S for *synonym,* A for *antonym,* and D for *different.*

_____ a. harmful

_____ b. questionable

_____ c. helpful

2. Distinguishing Fact from Opinion

Two of the statements below present *facts,* which can be proved correct. The other statement is an *opinion,* which expresses someone's thoughts or beliefs. Label the statements F for *fact* and O for *opinion.*

_____ a. Yogurt ingredients are milk and yogurt or yogurt starter.

_____ b. You can easily make cheese from yogurt in your own kitchen.

_____ c. You can buy yogurt starters in a supermarket.

3. **Keeping Events in Order**

   Label the statements below 1, 2, and 3 to show the order in which the events happened.

   _____ a. Drain the yogurt overnight.

   _____ b. Line a strainer or sieve with cheesecloth or paper towels.

   _____ c. Make yogurt.

4. **Making Correct Inferences**

   Two of the statements below are correct *inferences,* or reasonable guesses. They are based on information in the passage. The other statement is an incorrect, or faulty, inference. Label the statements C for *correct* inference and F for *faulty* inference.

   _____ a. Cheese making is too difficult for individuals.

   _____ b. Cheese making takes time and patience.

   _____ c. Cheese is made from the solids in milk.

5. **Understanding Main Ideas**

   One of the statements below expresses the main idea of the passage. One statement is too general, or too broad. The other explains only part of the passage; it is too narrow. Label the statements M for *main idea,* B for *too broad,* and N for *too narrow.*

   _____ a. Some cheese is easy to make.

   _____ b. Making cheese from yogurt begins with heating milk.

   _____ c. Making a simple cheese from yogurt teaches the basics of how cheese is made.

Correct Answers, Part A _____

Correct Answers, Part B _____

Total Correct Answers _____

King Alfred the Great

Without King Alfred of Wessex in southwestern England, the course of English history may have been quite different because he helped unite the nation. Before his time, England had been a land of small kingdoms, including four Saxon kingdoms of which Wessex was the strongest.

Born in about 848, Alfred was the youngest of King Ethelwulf's three sons, each of whom ruled the kingdom of Wessex. Alfred, who gained renown as a statesman and a warrior, was by temperament a scholar whose health was never robust.

Despite his health, Alfred fought with his brother Ethelred against Danish invaders, and after Ethelred died in 871, Alfred was acclaimed king. He had already won the confidence of the army and would justify their trust by becoming an outstanding wartime leader.

The Danes had penetrated all parts of England, including the other Saxon kingdoms, which had fallen to the invaders. Under Alfred's leadership, the Saxons bravely tried to stem the Danish invasion, but in 878 Alfred was defeated at Chippenham and was forced into hiding. A few months later, he forced the Danes to agree on a boundary between Alfred's kingdom and the Danish lands, called the Danelaw, to the north. The treaty, however, did not assure permanent peace, and the Danes attacked London and coastal towns repeatedly. In about 886, English forces finally defeated the Danes, and those who were not under the control of the Danes acknowledged Alfred as their leader. In time, the Saxon kingdoms began to merge into a single nation.

In addition to being the defender of his country, Alfred took a keen interest in law and order and the cultural development of his people. He rebuilt London, which had been partly destroyed by the Danes; collected and revised the old laws of the kingdom; and helped revived learning by inviting teachers and writers from other European countries to instruct the people. Under his guidance, scholars translated the great books from Latin to English and began to compile the *Anglo-Saxon Chronicle*, a major source of Anglo-Saxon history.

When Alfred died in 899, he was in no sense a true king of England, for he ruled less than half of the island. However, because of his outstanding leadership during times of war and peace, he became known as Alfred the Great and was the only English king in history to be bestowed with the honor of that title.

Reading Time _____

Recalling Facts

1. During Alfred's time, southern England
   - ❑ a. was Europe's ruling nation.
   - ❑ b. was part of Denmark.
   - ❑ c. consisted of small kingdoms.

2. Alfred became king following the rule of
   - ❑ a. his father, King Ethelwulf.
   - ❑ b. his brother, King Ethelred.
   - ❑ c. his uncle, King Wessex.

3. In 878, Alfred was defeated by the Danish
   - ❑ a. at London.
   - ❑ b. in Danelaw.
   - ❑ c. at Chippenham.

4. Under Alfred's leadership, the English finally defeated the Danes in
   - ❑ a. 877.
   - ❑ b. 886.
   - ❑ c. 899.

5. In England, the honor of the title "The Great" has been given to
   - ❑ a. all English kings before Alfred.
   - ❑ b. only Alfred.
   - ❑ c. all English kings since Alfred.

Understanding Ideas

6. According to the article, Alfred is considered
   - ❑ a. an admirable leader of his people.
   - ❑ b. England's most powerful king.
   - ❑ c. a true king of England.

7. Unlike the English kings who followed him, Alfred
   - ❑ a. was never acclaimed king.
   - ❑ b. did not rule the whole country.
   - ❑ c. was an effective leader during war and peace.

8. It is likely that without Alfred's leadership,
   - ❑ a. the Saxons would have defeated the Danes.
   - ❑ b. the Saxons would have been defeated by the Danes.
   - ❑ c. the English language would have disappeared.

9. A word that aptly describes Alfred is
   - ❑ a. divisive.
   - ❑ b. dynamic.
   - ❑ c. disillusioned.

10. If Alfred had not been king, he very likely would have been
    - ❑ a. a soldier.
    - ❑ b. an actor.
    - ❑ c. a scholar.

Viking Wolves

Fierce fighters from Norway and Denmark known as the Vikings tore into the British Isles like ravenous wolves. One of the first reported Viking attacks on England was on the island of Lindisfarne, which had been settled by monks who had chosen the island for its safety. For almost 350 years, the monks had lived quiet contemplative lives there, and then Viking raiders arrived in the year 793.

When he heard of the attack on Lindisfarne, a scholar wrote to Ethelred, king of Northumbria: " . . . never before has such a terror appeared in Britain as we have now suffered . . . , nor was it thought that such an inroad from the sea could be made."

A twelfth-century writer gave this account of the Viking raid on Lindisfarne: " . . . the pagans from the northern regions came with a naval force to Britain like stinging hornets and spread on all sides like fearful wolves, robbed, tore and slaughtered not only beasts of burden, sheep and oxen, but even . . . companies of monks and nuns. And they came to the church of Lindisfarne, laid everything waste with grievous plundering . . . and seized all the treasures of the holy church. They killed some of the brothers, took some away with them in fetters, many they drove out, . . . some they drowned in the sea."

1. Recognizing Words in Context

Find the word *ravenous* in the passage. One definition below is a *synonym* for that word; it means the same or almost the same. One definition is an *antonym*; it has the opposite or nearly opposite meaning. The other has a completely different meaning. Label the definitions S for *synonym*, A for *antonym*, and D for *different*.

_____ a. voracious

_____ b. colonized

_____ c. satiated

2. Distinguishing Fact from Opinion

Two of the statements below present *facts*, which can be proved correct. The other statement is an *opinion*, which expresses someone's thoughts or beliefs. Label the statements F for *fact* and O for *opinion*.

_____ a. The Viking attack on Lindisfarne was the worst terror the people of England had ever suffered.

_____ b. Viking raiders attacked the island of Lindisfarne in the year 793.

_____ c. The Vikings killed animals and people on the island of Lindisfarne.

3. Keeping Events in Order

Label the statements below 1, 2, and 3 to show the order in which the events happened.

_____ a. Viking raiders attacked Lindisfarne.

_____ b. Monks settled on the island of Lindisfarne.

_____ c. Many monks were killed; others were driven away or carried off.

4. Making Correct Inferences

Two of the statements below are correct *inferences*, or reasonable guesses. They are based on information in the passage. The other statement is an incorrect, or faulty, inference. Label the statements C for *correct* inference and F for *faulty* inference.

_____ a. Viking attacks were directed mostly at communities of monks and nuns.

_____ b. The monks on the island of Lindisfarne expected to live in peace.

_____ c. The islanders were not prepared for the Viking attack.

5. Understanding Main Ideas

One of the statements below expresses the main idea of the passage. One statement is too general, or too broad. The other explains only part of the passage; it is too narrow. Label the statements M for *main idea,* B for *too broad,* and N for *too narrow.*

_____ a. Viking raiders plundered the treasures of the church of Lindisfarne.

_____ b. Beginning in the late eighth century, Viking raiders staged a series of attacks on the British Isles.

_____ c. One of the first reported Viking attacks on England was on the island of Lindisfarne, which monks had settled.

Correct Answers, Part A _____

Correct Answers, Part B _____

Total Correct Answers _____

3 | A | Abraham, Father of Faith

Abraham, considered the patriarch of the Jewish, Christian, and Islamic faiths, is one of the major figures in the history of religion. Applied to Abraham, the term *patriarch* means that he was considered the founding father of the nation of Israel.

What is known about Abraham is found only in Genesis, the first book of the Bible, which is the sacred scriptures, or writings, of the Judeo-Christian religions. Genesis states that Abraham was a native of Ur in southern Mesopotamia. He was probably the head of a large clan of people who lived a seminomadic existence. For some reason, the clan moved northward and settled near Haran, where Abraham received a call from God, telling him to leave his homeland and go to a new location that would be revealed to him.

In addition to commanding him to move, God made Abraham a promise: "I will make of thee a great nation." According to scriptures, God's arrangement with Abraham, called a covenant, would be kept if Abraham obeyed God's directive, and his people remained faithful to God. This was the first covenant, or solemn agreement, that God made with the nation of Israel, and it is this covenant to which Israel owes its origin as a nation.

Abraham kept his part of the bargain, and he and his clan left Haran and traveled through Syria to Canaan, or the area that is present-day Israel. This was to be Israel's Promised Land.

Once Abraham and his clan were settled in Canaan, God renewed his covenant and promised that He would give Abraham descendants. Because Abraham and his wife, Sarah, were already quite old, they were doubtful that they would ever have a child. So Abraham fathered a son, Ishmael, with Sarah's slave, Hagar. After Ishmael was born, Sarah and Abraham had a son, Isaac, who, according to Genesis, was to be the heir through whom the covenant would continue.

Late in life, after Sarah had died, Abraham married a woman named Catarrh and with her had many children. These other children were rewarded with an inheritance when they grew up and were then sent away from Canaan to live elsewhere. Isaac alone inherited the Promised Land, and after Isaac's death, the land went to his son, Jacob, whose name God changed to Israel. Abraham, the father of Israel, died at the age of 175 and was buried next to Sarah.

Reading Time _____

Recalling Facts

1. Applied to Abraham, the term *patriarch* means that he
   - ❏ a. was the head of a large clan of people.
   - ❏ b. is considered a founding father of the nation of Israel.
   - ❏ c. had many children.

2. What is known about Abraham comes from
   - ❏ a. the first book of the Bible.
   - ❏ b. the last book of the Bible.
   - ❏ c. oral tradition.

3. Israel became a nation because of
   - ❏ a. the renaming of Ur.
   - ❏ b. God's covenant with Israel.
   - ❏ c. Abraham's inheritance.

4. The area now known as Israel was once called
   - ❏ a. Genesis.
   - ❏ b. Haran.
   - ❏ c. Canaan.

5. The Promised Land was inherited by
   - ❏ a. Sarah.
   - ❏ b. Ishmael.
   - ❏ c. Isaac.

Understanding Ideas

6. You can conclude from the article that God made a covenant with Abraham because Abraham was
   - ❏ a. a trustworthy person.
   - ❏ b. the father of Judaism.
   - ❏ c. a major religious figure.

7. Abraham's willingness to obey God shows that Abraham
   - ❏ a. had faith.
   - ❏ b. was superstitious.
   - ❏ c. had no strong roots.

8. From the article, you can conclude that the covenant God made with Abraham was
   - ❏ a. the only covenant God made with the people of Israel.
   - ❏ b. one of several covenants God made with Israel.
   - ❏ c. the last covenant God made with Israel.

9. It is likely that the nation of Israel got its name from
   - ❏ a. the name God gave to Jacob.
   - ❏ b. an old Hebrew legend.
   - ❏ c. a book in the Bible.

10. God promised Abraham, "I will make of thee a great nation." This means that
    - ❏ a. Abraham would become a major political figure.
    - ❏ b. Abraham's descendants would be the foundation of a new country.
    - ❏ c. all of the world's religions would begin with Abraham.

According to the Bible, the tribes of Israel passed over the Jordan River and settled in the land of Canaan after many years of wandering in the desert. Having done so, they began to storm and capture the Canaanite city-states. The first to fall was Jericho. Joshua, the Israelites' leader, and his troops tumbled the city's walls with mighty blasts on trumpets.

Archaeologists have found evidence of the fiery destruction of Canaanite cities in the late thirteenth and early twelfth centuries B.C. New settlements controlled by Israelites were built on the ruins. Archaeologists have also found the remains of Israelite villages on other sites, and their discoveries suggest that the Israelites probably did not come into Canaan in a single body as the Bible states. It is more likely that they trickled in over many years, tribe by tribe or clan by clan. After they built up strength and numbers, the Israelites challenged the local powers.

By the time the Israelites arrived in Canaan, the Canaanite city-states had grown weak and relied heavily on the Egyptians and the Hittites for protection. However, both of those powers had become occupied in fighting off their own enemies. Canaan lost its protectors and was ripe for plucking by the Israelites.

1. **Recognizing Words in Context**

   Find the word *storm* in the passage. One definition below is a *synonym* for that word; it means the same or almost the same. One definition is an *antonym;* it has the opposite or nearly opposite meaning. The other has a completely different meaning. Label the definitions S for *synonym*, A for *antonym,* and D for *different.*

   _____ a. rain

   _____ b. protect

   _____ c. attack

2. **Distinguishing Fact from Opinion**

   Two of the statements below present *facts,* which can be proved correct. The other statement is an *opinion,* which expresses someone's thoughts or beliefs. Label the statements F for *fact* and O for *opinion.*

   _____ a. Israelite settlements were built on ruined Canaanite cities.

   _____ b. Israelites probably did not come into Canaan in a single body.

   _____ c. The Canaanite cities were destroyed in the thirteenth and twelfth centuries B.C.

3. Keeping Events in Order

Label the statements below 1, 2, and 3 to show the order in which the events happened.

_____ a. The Israelites passed over the Jordan River and entered the land of Canaan.

_____ b. The Israelites conquered the land of Canaan.

_____ c. The Egyptians and the Hittites stopped protecting the Canaanites.

4. Making Correct Inferences

Two of the statements below are correct *inferences,* or reasonable guesses. They are based on information in the passage. The other statement is an incorrect, or faulty, inference. Label the statements C for *correct* inference and F for *faulty* inference.

_____ a. The Israelites grew stronger than the Canaanites.

_____ b. The conquest of Canaan would probably not have been possible if the Egyptians and Hittites had continued to protect it.

_____ c. All the Bible's stories are true.

5. Understanding Main Ideas

One of the statements below expresses the main idea of the passage. One statement is too general, or too broad. The other explains only part of the passage; it is too narrow. Label the statements M for *main idea,* B for *too broad,* and N for *too narrow.*

_____ a. The story of the Israelites begins thousands of years ago.

_____ b. The Israelites entered and conquered the land of Canaan.

_____ c. Jericho was the first Canaanite city-state to fall to the Israelites.

Correct Answers, Part A _____

Correct Answers, Part B _____

Total Correct Answers _____

24

White and Bright

The process of whitening a substance by removing its natural coloring is called bleaching. Some bleaching is done in the home, but the main use of bleach is in industry. Fibers, cloth, paper pulp, sugar, and flour are often bleached during manufacturing. In the home, bleach added to laundry water helps remove dirt and restore whiteness or brightness to fabrics. Some people use a bleaching agent cosmetically to lighten the color of their hair.

Two chemical processes can be used in bleaching. Oxidation involves combining oxygen with a substance. Reduction is the removal of an oxygen molecule from a compound.

Common oxidizing bleaches include sodium perborate, a relatively mild material that can be used on all fibers. Hydrogen peroxide is a somewhat stronger chemical that is widely employed for commercial bleaching of cotton and for lightening hair. Sodium hypochlorite is the familiar chlorine bleach used in the home, and because it both disinfects and bleaches, sodium hypochlorite can be used on heavily soiled garments such as diapers and on hospital laundry.

An oxidizing agent was once used to bleach sugar, but now sugar is bleached with complex substances called ion-exchange resins. Paper mills lighten pulp in a multistage process that employs liquid and gaseous chlorine, a highly toxic substance.

Three common reducing bleaches, which are safe on all fabrics, but not on all colors, are sodium bisulfite, sodium hydrosulfite, and titanium stripper. The sulfurous acid used in bleaching wool also works by reduction. Reducing bleaches are commonly used in many dry-cleaning stores, as are some oxidizing bleaches.

Optical bleaches, or brighteners, are composed of certain organic compounds that can absorb ultraviolet light and emit a blue light. Used on fabrics, these substances will make a yellowed garment look white. For this reason, they are added to many household detergents. Clothing saturated with them glows brightly in ultraviolet light, or black light.

Sunlight is the oldest known bleaching agent. The ancient Hebrews and Egyptians dipped their fabrics in water and set them out in the sun to bleach. In Ireland, Scotland, and Belgium, fine linens are still bleached by a similar method. Bleaching powder was introduced in 1799 by the Scottish chemist Charles Tennant. It was easier and safer to use on fabrics than the chlorine gas it replaced. The relative importance of bleaching powders decreased in the mid-1900s with the development of more advanced liquid and solid bleaching agents.

Reading Time _____

Recalling Facts

1. The main use of bleach is
   - ❏ a. in the home.
   - ❏ b. in industry.
   - ❏ c. on fabrics.

2. Oxidation involves combining a substance with
   - ❏ a. bleach.
   - ❏ b. chemicals.
   - ❏ c. oxygen.

3. The two chemical processes used in bleaching are oxidation and
   - ❏ a. reduction.
   - ❏ b. addition.
   - ❏ c. attraction.

4. The oldest known bleaching agent is
   - ❏ a. chlorine.
   - ❏ b. sunlight.
   - ❏ c. sodium bisulfite.

5. The bleach used for lightening hair is
   - ❏ a. hydrogen peroxide.
   - ❏ b. sodium hypochlorite.
   - ❏ c. sodium bisulfite.

Understanding Ideas

6. You can conclude from the article that industrial bleaches are
   - ❏ a. stronger than home bleaches.
   - ❏ b. milder than home bleaches.
   - ❏ c. used cosmetically.

7. According to the article, a blue shirt
   - ❏ a. should never be washed using reducing bleaches.
   - ❏ b. might be washable using reducing bleaches.
   - ❏ c. should be washed using optical bleaches.

8. You can conclude from the article that a fine linen
   - ❏ a. should never be bleached.
   - ❏ b. could safely be bleached with sodium bisulfite.
   - ❏ c. could be bleached with any bleaching agent.

9. The article suggests that liquid and solid bleaching agents are
   - ❏ a. more effective than bleaching powders.
   - ❏ b. being replaced by new types of bleaches.
   - ❏ c. used mainly in dry-cleaning stores.

10. The article wants you to understand that the bleaching process
    - ❏ a. is vital to our health.
    - ❏ b. makes most products safer.
    - ❏ c. makes some substances more attractive.

Just a Little Lighter

Some people experiment with lemon juice, peroxide, and sunlight to bleach their hair—sometimes with good results, sometimes not. If you decide to lighten your hair and opt to have a professional hairdresser do the job, what happens during the process?

Before the hairdresser applies the bleaching agent, your hair is shampooed so that any dirt and oil on the scalp or in the hair won't keep the bleach from doing its job. Each hair is made up of overlapping cells, something like the shingles on a roof. When it is applied to the hair, the bleaching agent causes the cells to expand. Then the agent slips under the cells into the hair shaft and strips the hair of its color. The hairdresser carefully times how long the bleaching agent remains on your hair and rinses it out when the desired amount of lightening is achieved.

If you bleach your hair too often, the hair cells can't recover. Frequent lifting and lowering of the little "shingles" can cause them to break. Getting a permanent and a new color at the same time is also very hard on the hair because the chemicals react with each other. Hairdressers call this reaction overprocessing. Have you heard about someone whose hair turned green or fell out because of bleaching? That's the result of overprocessing. But used correctly, today's hair-bleaching products are safe.

1. Recognizing Words in Context

Find the word *opt* in the passage. One definition below is a *synonym* for that word; it means the same or almost the same. One definition is an *antonym;* it has the opposite or nearly opposite meaning. The other has a completely different meaning. Label the definitions S for *synonym,* A for *antonym,* and D for *different.*

_____ a. choose

_____ b. believe

_____ c. reject

2. Distinguishing Fact from Opinion

Two of the statements below present *facts,* which can be proved correct. The other statement is an *opinion,* which expresses someone's thoughts or beliefs. Label the statements F for *fact* and O for *opinion.*

_____ a. Today's hair-bleaching products are safe.

_____ b. Hair is made up of overlapping cells.

_____ c. The bleaching agent causes cells to expand.

3. **Keeping Events in Order**

Label the statements below 1, 2, and 3 to show the order in which the events happened.

_____ a. Hair cells expand.

_____ b. The bleach removes the color from the hair shaft.

_____ c. The hairdresser applies the bleaching agent.

4. **Making Correct Inferences**

Two of the statements below are correct *inferences,* or reasonable guesses. They are based on information in the passage. The other statement is an incorrect, or faulty, inference. Label the statements C for *correct* inference and F for *faulty* inference.

_____ a. Do-it-yourself bleaching is less accurate than professional hair coloring.

_____ b. Bleaching is always bad for the hair.

_____ c. Hair bleaching involves a chemical process.

5. **Understanding Main Ideas**

One of the statements below expresses the main idea of the passage. One statement is too general, or too broad. The other explains only part of the passage; it is too narrow. Label the statements M for *main idea,* B for *too broad,* and N for *too narrow.*

_____ a. Bleaching agents cause hair cells to expand, allowing the bleach to act on the hair shaft.

_____ b. Bleaching changes hair color.

_____ c. Hair bleach works by changing the hair chemically and physically.

Correct Answers, Part A _____

Correct Answers, Part B _____

Total Correct Answers _____

The field of design goes beyond painting and drawing, sculpture, architecture, and handicrafts. It includes thousands of mass-produced objects that were designed for everyday use. Many industrial designers' products, from chairs to stereo equipment, are exhibited in art museums.

Throughout the ages, people have designed things to meet their varying needs. The armor worn by knights was designed to protect them in medieval warfare. Birch bark canoes were designed to meet the mobility needs of the American Indians. Skyscrapers were designed to conserve valuable ground space.

As new materials and methods are developed, designs are created to make use of them, and as needs change, new or improved designs are made to meet those needs. Today's standard telephone could not have been designed 100 years ago. The modern telephone, with swift automatic dialing, is convenient to use, and its design makes it usable and compact. The modern telephone, housed in strong plastic with smooth and easy-to-clean surfaces that come in a variety of colors, blends into the decor of homes and businesses.

The first step in the modern design of any object is to consider its use, which helps determine its shape, material, color, and size. Objects designed for use, or with functional design, have no needless ornamentation, and their parts are large enough to function properly and effectively but no larger. Modern functional design appears in many homes, especially in the kitchen, where the clean, simple lines of appliances offer beauty as the appliances themselves help save work. Manufacturers of refrigerators, stoves, and washing machines combine the talents of fine engineers and designers to produce machines that are beautiful as well as useful.

People are slower to accept improved designs in some home furnishings, however. The common dining-room chair, for example, is often still made of straight slabs of wood. Its shape has little in common with the shape of the human body, and after a time, it becomes uncomfortable. Designers have been developing lightweight chairs that conform to the natural curves of the body and support it with ease and comfort. The molded plywood chair designed by Charles Eames in 1940 is a classic of contemporary design.

Good design extends to the styling of clothes, the sleek aerodynamic lines of automobiles, the patterns of superhighways, and the planning of growing cities. In these and in other areas, people use their creative abilities to design things for better living.

Reading Time _____

Recalling Facts

1. Mass-produced designer objects are usually intended for
   - ❏ a. museum exhibits.
   - ❏ b. display only.
   - ❏ c. everyday use.

2. Design for use is
   - ❏ a. limited design.
   - ❏ b. functional design.
   - ❏ c. classic design.

3. Charles Eames is known for designing
   - ❏ a. heavy dining room chairs.
   - ❏ b. comfortable, lightweight chairs.
   - ❏ c. a new line of kitchen products.

4. People are slow to accept improved design in
   - ❏ a. home furnishings.
   - ❏ b. kitchen appliances.
   - ❏ c. clothing.

5. Birch bark canoes met American Indians'
   - ❏ a. need for protection during warfare.
   - ❏ b. communication needs.
   - ❏ c. mobility needs.

Understanding Ideas

6. People probably prefer everyday objects that are
   - ❏ a. attractive as well as functional.
   - ❏ b. more functional than attractive.
   - ❏ c. more attractive than functional.

7. The article suggests that contemporary industrial design
   - ❏ a. varies little from past design.
   - ❏ b. is more desirable than designs of the past.
   - ❏ c. is less desirable than designs of the past.

8. From the article, you can conclude that today's standard telephone
   - ❏ a. is less colorful than earlier telephones.
   - ❏ b. has a more ornate design than earlier telephones.
   - ❏ c. is easier to use than earlier telephones.

9. The purpose of product design should be to
   - ❏ a. follow design formulas.
   - ❏ b. copy the past.
   - ❏ c. improve the quality of living.

10. You can conclude from the article that most people decorate their living rooms with
    - ❏ a. traditionally designed furnishings.
    - ❏ b. furnishings with functional designs.
    - ❏ c. furnishings with contemporary designs.

Designing President

Thomas Jefferson was the third president of the United States, the principal
author of the Declaration of Independence, and a founder of the University of
Virginia. He was also a talented designer whose interest in furniture and architecture extended to designing his own home—Monticello in Virginia—inside
and out. Monticello contained many examples of his practical ideas.

Jefferson installed a dumbwaiter—a small elevator with shelves—to carry
wine from the wine cellar to the dining room. He designed portable serving
tables so that guests could help themselves without having their conversation
interrupted by servants.

One of his creations was a four-sided music stand that enabled up to five
musicians to play from the same stand. It folded up into a compact box when
it was not in use. He also designed a combination swivel chair, lounge, and
writing table, on which he surely produced much of his correspondence while
at Monticello.

In 1792 Jefferson anonymously submitted a design for the President's
House—later known as the White House—but his design was not accepted.
Jefferson felt that the design chosen was far too grand for the new country.
He described it as "big enough for two emperors, one pope, and the high
Lama"!

1. Recognizing Words in Context

Find the word *grand* in the passage.
One definition below is a *synonym* for
that word; it means the same or
almost the same. One definition is an
antonym; it has the opposite or nearly
opposite meaning. The other has a
completely different meaning. Label
the definitions S for *synonym,* A for
antonym, and D for *different.*

_____ a. inferior

_____ b. magnificent

_____ c. foremost

2. Distinguishing Fact from Opinion

Two of the statements below present
facts, which can be proved correct.
The other statement is an *opinion,*
which expresses someone's thoughts
or beliefs. Label the statements F for
fact and O for *opinion.*

_____ a. The design chosen for the
President's House was far
too grand for the new
country.

_____ b. Jefferson designed his own
home in Virginia.

_____ c. Jefferson's design for the
President's House was not
accepted.

3. Keeping Events in Order

Label the statements below 1, 2, and 3 to show the order in which the events happened.

_____ a. Jefferson anonymously submitted a design for the President's House.

_____ b. Jefferson's design was rejected.

_____ c. Jefferson described the President's House as "big enough for two emperors."

4. Making Correct Inferences

Two of the statements below are correct *inferences*, or reasonable guesses. They are based on information in the passage. The other statement is an incorrect, or faulty, inference. Label the statements C for *correct* inference and F for *faulty* inference.

_____ a. Thomas Jefferson was a person with many talents.

_____ b. Jefferson's design was rejected because it was not good.

_____ c. Thomas Jefferson did not like the design chosen for the President's House.

5. Understanding Main Ideas

One of the statements below expresses the main idea of the passage. One statement is too general, or too broad. The other explains only part of the passage; it is too narrow. Label the statements M for *main idea*, B for *too broad*, and N for *too narrow*.

_____ a. Thomas Jefferson, third president of the United States, was talented in furniture design and architecture.

_____ b. Thomas Jefferson installed a dumbwaiter—a small elevator with shelves.

_____ c. For many reasons, Thomas Jefferson was one of this country's finest presidents.

Correct Answers, Part A _____

Correct Answers, Part B _____

Total Correct Answers _____

6 A Genghis Khan

The origin of the Mongols is unknown, but the earliest reference to them by name is in a document of the Chinese T'ang Dynasty, which lasted from 618 to 907. By the thirteenth century, the nomadic tribes of Mongols had become a powerful military force. Under the leadership of Genghis Khan and his successors, the Mongols established an empire that reached from present-day China and Korea in the east to Eastern Europe and the shores of the Mediterranean Sea in the west.

In 1206 Temujin was elected head of a federation of Mongol tribes, and his title within the league became Genghis Khan. Between 1206 and 1225, the Mongols conquered a dominion that stretched from the China Sea to the Caspian. On the north, it bordered the forest belt of Siberia, and on the south, it touched the Pamir range in Tibet and the central plains of China.

By 1215 all of northern China, including the capital at Ta-tu (present-day Beijing), had been taken. In 1218 the Mongols moved into eastern Turkestan. Between 1219 and 1225, they added western Turkestan, and advance troops penetrated into southern Russia and raided cities in the Crimea.

The Mongol Empire built by Genghis Khan was not a unified state but a vast collection of territories held together by military force. Because it was controlled by so many military leaders, all theoretically answering to the great khan, the empire carried within it the seeds of its own breakdown.

Central power rested with the khan and his councilors. Although they were well organized militarily, the Mongols had no developed concept for ruling settled populations. The various territories were under the authority of military commanders, and new conquests were not administered, just economically exploited. In areas that were under subjugation longer, there was some growth of administration. Local bureaucracies, though dominated by Mongols, usually followed administrative patterns that had been locally developed. This was especially true in China, with its ancient and vast bureaucracy.

While Genghis Khan was still living, he divided the empire among his four favorite sons. Genghis Khan and his eldest son, Juchi, both died in 1227. At a convocation of Mongol leaders, Ogadai was appointed supreme khan. Ogadai made his capital at Karakorum in central Mongolia, and he immediately set out to add more of China to the Mongol conquests. By 1234 all but the southernmost region of China had been occupied and incorporated.

Reading Time _____

Recalling Facts

1. Mongols were
   - ❑ a. Chinese bureaucrats.
   - ❑ b. nomadic tribes.
   - ❑ c. Korean military forces.

2. The Mongol Empire was
   - ❑ a. a large, unified state.
   - ❑ b. a huge bureaucracy.
   - ❑ c. a vast collection of territories.

3. Genghis Khan was elected to head the Mongol federation in
   - ❑ a. 907.
   - ❑ b. 1206.
   - ❑ c. 1237.

4. Genghis Khan was the title of
   - ❑ a. Ogadai.
   - ❑ b. Juchi.
   - ❑ c. Temujin.

5. Ogadai set up his capital at
   - ❑ a. Ta-tu.
   - ❑ b. Karakorum.
   - ❑ c. Turkestan.

Understanding Ideas

6. The article suggests that the Mongol Empire was established by
   - ❑ a. democratic process.
   - ❑ b. military power.
   - ❑ c. inheritance.

7. You can conclude from the article that the cause of the Mongols' downfall was
   - ❑ a. Genghis Khan's death.
   - ❑ b. the occupation of China.
   - ❑ c. the lack of a unified state.

8. You can conclude that after Genghis Khan's death, the Mongol Empire
   - ❑ a. became more powerful.
   - ❑ b. collapsed.
   - ❑ c. became more unified.

9. The article suggests that the Mongol commanders were
   - ❑ a. strong local administrators.
   - ❑ b. weak local administrators.
   - ❑ c. did not serve as administrators.

10. The article wants you to understand that Genghis Khan
    - ❑ a. was a great administrator.
    - ❑ b. conquered the world.
    - ❑ c. was a brilliant military leader.

Kublai Kahn

Two generations after the Mongol ruler Genghis Khan began his conquest of China, his grandson, Kublai Khan, came to the throne. Born in 1216, Kublai Khan became khan in 1256 on the death of his father. Kublai Khan set out to finish the conquest of China that his grandfather had begun and his father had continued.

Kublai Khan established his capital at Cambaluc and built a royal city there. Today, the modern city of Beijing stands on that site. In 1271 Kublai Khan received at his court the young European adventurer Marco Polo. Polo remained in China for seventeen years, traveling where no European had ever been before and where few would journey for centuries after. A favorite of the khan's court, Polo often officially toured the empire for the khan and even served as a city governor for three years.

By 1279 Kublai Khan had completed his conquest of China and founded the Mongol dynasty that ruled China for many generations. An able administrator, Kublai Khan ruled over a vast empire that included what is present-day China, Mongolia, and Myanmar, and across Tibet, Central Asia, and parts of Russia. He died in 1294, the undisputed ruler of the East.

11. Recognizing Words in Context

Find the word *undisputed* in the passage. One definition below is a *synonym* for that word; it means the same or almost the same. One definition is an *antonym;* it has the opposite or nearly opposite meaning. The other has a completely different meaning. Label the definitions S for *synonym*, A for *antonym*, and D for *different*.

_____ a. deposed

_____ b. uncontested

_____ c. debated

2. Distinguishing Fact from Opinion

Two of the statements below present *facts,* which can be proved correct. The other statement is an *opinion,* which expresses someone's thoughts or beliefs. Label the statements F for *fact* and O for *opinion.*

_____ a. Kublai Kahn was Genghis Kahn's grandson.

_____ b. Kublai Kahn's empire included parts of Russia.

_____ c. Kublai Kahn was an able ruler.

3. Keeping Events in Order

Label the statements below 1, 2, and 3 to show the order in which the events happened.

_____ a. By 1279 Kublai Khan had completed his conquest of China.

_____ b. Kublai Khan inherited the throne from his father.

_____ c. Marco Polo visited the Khan's court.

4. Making Correct Inferences

Two of the statements below are correct *inferences,* or reasonable guesses. They are based on information in the passage. The other statement is an incorrect, or faulty, inference. Label the statements C for *correct* inference and F for *faulty* inference.

_____ a. Kublai Khan was important in China's history.

_____ b. Kublai Khan was a strong ruler.

_____ c. Marco Polo was responsible for Kublai Khan's success.

5. Understanding Main Ideas

One of the statements below expresses the main idea of the passage. One statement is too general, or too broad. The other explains only part of the passage; it is too narrow. Label the statements M for *main idea,* B for *too broad,* and N for *too narrow.*

_____ a. Kublai Kahn received young Marco Polo, the European adventurer, at his court.

_____ b. Kublai Kahn was one of China's most powerful and successful rulers.

_____ c. China's history goes back many centuries.

Correct Answers, Part A _____

Correct Answers, Part B _____

Total Correct Answers _____

Settling Down

The one factor that made it possible for humans to settle in permanent communities was agriculture. After farming was developed in the Middle East in about 6500 B.C., people living in tribes or family units did not have to be on the move continually searching for food or herding their animals. Once people could control the production of food and be assured of a reliable annual supply of it, their lives changed completely.

People began to found permanent communities in fertile river valleys, and settlers learned to use the readily available water supply to irrigate the land. Being settled in one place made it possible to domesticate animals that could be used as sources of food and clothing.

Farming was a revolutionary discovery, which not only made a reliable food supply available but also made settlements possible. With more food available, more people could be fed, and populations, therefore, increased. The growing number of people meant that more people were available to work, and this led to the development of more complex social structures and specialized workers. With a food surplus, a community could support a variety of workers who were not farmers.

Farming has always relied on a dependable water supply from rivers and streams or regular precipitation. The first great civilizations grew up along rivers, but later communities were able to develop by taking advantage of the rainy seasons.

All of the ancient civilizations probably developed in much the same way, in spite of regional and climatic differences. As villages grew, the accumulation of more numerous and substantial goods became possible. Heavier pottery could replace animal-skin gourds as containers for food. Cloth could be woven from wool and flax. Permanent structures made of wood, brick, and stone could be erected.

The science of mathematics was an early outgrowth of agriculture. People studied the movements of the moon, sun, and planets to calculate seasons. In so doing, they created the first calendars that they used to calculate the arrival of each growing season. Measurement of land areas was necessary if property was to be divided accurately. Measurements of amounts of seeds or grains was also a factor in farming and housekeeping.

The use of measuring led naturally to record keeping, and for record keeping some form of writing was necessary. The earliest civilizations all seem to have used picture writing. The pictures represented both sounds and objects to the reader.

Reading Time _____

Recalling Facts

1. Agriculture made it possible for humans to
   - ❏ a. settle in permanent communities.
   - ❏ b. herd animals.
   - ❏ c. keep records.

2. Farming has always relied on a
   - ❏ a. reliable food supply.
   - ❏ b. dependable water supply.
   - ❏ c. large work force.

3. Early people studied the movements of the moon, sun, and planets in order to
   - ❏ a. predict the future.
   - ❏ b. calculate the seasons.
   - ❏ c. determine the weather.

4. The earliest civilizations wrote by using
   - ❏ a. an alphabet.
   - ❏ b. rock formations.
   - ❏ c. pictures.

5. Early writing represented
   - ❏ a. sounds and objects.
   - ❏ b. sounds.
   - ❏ c. objects.

Understanding Ideas

6. The development of agriculture
   - ❏ a. led to a decrease in populations.
   - ❏ b. meant people no longer relied on animals for food.
   - ❏ c. made early civilizations possible.

7. Before the development of farming, people
   - ❏ a. moved about in search of food.
   - ❏ b. did not live in family units.
   - ❏ c. lived in permanent settlements.

8. You can conclude that people in early farming civilizations
   - ❏ a. studied mathematics.
   - ❏ b. had no practical use for mathematics.
   - ❏ c. had no knowledge of mathematics.

9. Calendars were important because they
   - ❏ a. revealed the movement of the planets.
   - ❏ b. predicted the weather.
   - ❏ c. helped farmers determine when to plant crops.

10. You can conclude from the article that most early advances were the result of
    - ❏ a. advanced education.
    - ❏ b. domesticating animals.
    - ❏ c. people living in permanent communities.

Corn and American Culture

Early in prehistory, Central American people began to domesticate wild grains. One of their most successful efforts was the cultivation of corn.

As people settled into villages, corn cultivation spread north throughout present-day Mexico. Corn was so vital to the culture of Central Americans that many tribes developed religious rituals for ensuring bountiful corn crops and celebrating harvests. Legends tell of a supernatural hero who cared for the first people by teaching them how to plant corn.

Well before Columbus and other Europeans arrived in the Americas, the cultivation of corn had spread across North America. Later, corn became a food staple for European settlers. A successful corn crop enabled the Massachusetts Pilgrims and other early colonists to survive.

The corn, also called maize, grown by early American Indians was not the corn that is cultivated today. Their field corn matured into large, tough kernels that they pounded into flour or ground into meal to make corn cakes and flat breads like tortillas. Sweet corn, the kind of corn that people enjoy as a vegetable, was developed from that tough Indian corn in the early nineteenth century. But corn remains closely tied to modern American culture. Americans traditionally celebrate their summer feast days, such as the Fourth of July and Labor Day, by eating the American vegetable, corn.

1. Recognizing Words in Context

Find the word *domesticate* in the passage. One definition below is a *synonym* for that word; it means the same or almost the same. One definition is an *antonym;* it has the opposite or nearly opposite meaning. The other has a completely different meaning. Label the definitions S for *synonym,* A for *antonym,* and D for *different.*

_____ a. tame

_____ b. unleash

_____ c. devour

2. Distinguishing Fact from Opinion

Two of the statements below present *facts,* which can be proved correct. The other statement is an *opinion,* which expresses someone's thoughts or beliefs. Label the statements F for *fact* and O for *opinion.*

_____ a. Sweet corn was developed from the American Indians' field corn.

_____ b. Corn spread across North America before Europeans came to the Americas.

_____ c. Corn remains closely tied to modern American culture.

3. Keeping Events in Order

Label the statements below 1, 2, and 3 to show the order in which the events happened.

_____ a. Many Central Americans developed rituals and legends associated with corn.

_____ b. People in Central America began to grow corn.

_____ c. Sweet corn was developed.

4. Making Correct Inferences

Two of the statements below are correct *inferences,* or reasonable guesses. They are based on information in the passage. The other statement is an incorrect, or faulty, inference. Label the statements C for *correct* inference and F for *faulty* inference.

_____ a. Native American corn was not good to eat.

_____ b. Corn has cultural significance as well as food value.

_____ c. Corn is a healthful and useful food.

5. Understanding Main Ideas

One of the statements below expresses the main idea of the passage. One statement is too general, or too broad. The other explains only part of the passage; it is too narrow. Label the statements M for *main idea,* B for *too broad,* and N for *too narrow.*

_____ a. Well before Europeans arrived in the Americas, the cultivation of corn had spread across North America.

_____ b. From ancient times, corn has been an important factor in American culture.

_____ c. Corn growing is an ancient activity.

Correct Answers, Part A _____

Correct Answers, Part B _____

Total Correct Answers _____

Mercury, the planet nearest the sun, is difficult to observe from the Earth because it rises and sets within two hours of the sun. Consequently, little was known about the planet until the Mariner 10 spacecraft made several flybys in 1974 and 1975.

Planetary scientists can estimate the age of a planet's surface by the number of impact craters on it. In general, the older the surface, the more craters it has. Some regions on Mercury are heavily cratered, suggesting that they are very old surfaces that were probably formed about 4 billion years ago. Between these regions are areas of gently rolling plains that may have been smoothed by volcanic lava flows or by accumulated deposits of fine material ejected during impacts. These plains are also old enough to have accumulated a large number of impact craters. Elsewhere on the planet are smooth, flat plains that are probably younger and volcanic in origin. These plains have relatively few impact craters. Sometime between the formation of the intercrater plains and the formation of the smooth plains, the whole planet may have shrunk as it cooled, causing the crust to buckle and form the long, steep cliffs called scarps.

The largest impact basin on Mercury has a diameter of about 800 miles (1,300 kilometers) and is surrounded by mountains that rise to heights of about 1.2 miles (2 kilometers). The crater was probably created by the impact of a large planetesimal when Mercury was forming. On the opposite side of the planet is an area of hilly, linear terrain that probably resulted from seismic waves caused by the same impact.

Like other airless, solid bodies in the solar system, the entire surface of Mercury is covered with a layer of rubble called regolith, which is composed of material, ranging from dust to boulders, that was scattered when impact craters were formed. This debris was in turn broken up and redistributed by subsequent impacts.

Mercury is very dense and has a magnetic field that is about 1 percent as strong as Earth's. This suggests the existence of a planetary core composed of iron and nickel and constituting about 40 percent of the planet's volume. The surface gravity is about one-third as strong as Earth's, and a thin atmosphere surrounds the planet. Radar images taken of Mercury in 1991 show what are considered to be large ice patches at the planet's north pole.

Reading Time _____

Recalling Facts

1. Mercury is the planet
   - ❏ a. closest to Earth.
   - ❏ b. farthest from the sun.
   - ❏ c. nearest the sun.

2. Scientists estimate the age of a planet's surface by
   - ❏ a. volcanic lava flows.
   - ❏ b. its magnetic field.
   - ❏ c. the number of impact craters on it.

3. The layer of rubble covering Mercury is called
   - ❏ a. scarp.
   - ❏ b. regolith.
   - ❏ c. impact stone.

4. The largest impact crater on Mercury is about
   - ❏ a. 800 miles (1,300 kilometers) across.
   - ❏ b. 1.2 miles (2 kilometers) across.
   - ❏ c. 20 miles (32 kilometers) across.

5. Mercury's ancient surfaces have
   - ❏ a. no impact craters.
   - ❏ b. many impact craters.
   - ❏ c. few impact craters.

Understanding Ideas

6. You can conclude that Mercury's nearness to the sun makes it extremely
   - ❏ a. windy.
   - ❏ b. humid.
   - ❏ c. hot.

7. It is likely that the climate on Mercury would
   - ❏ a. discourage life.
   - ❏ b. encourage life.
   - ❏ c. have no effect on life.

8. The article suggests that Mariner 10 was sent to observe Mercury because
   - ❏ a. Jupiter was too far away.
   - ❏ b. signs of life had been observed there.
   - ❏ c. little could be observed from the Earth.

9. Large ice patches were observed on Mercury's north pole, which suggests that
   - ❏ a. Mercury is a very wet planet.
   - ❏ b. the north pole faces away from the sun.
   - ❏ c. rainfall is frequent on the north pole.

10. Mercury's gravity is about one-third as strong as Earth's, which means that on Mercury people would weigh
    - ❏ a. less.
    - ❏ b. more.
    - ❏ c. about the same.

We owe much of our knowledge of the planet Mercury to the space probe Mariner 10, launched by the National Aeronautics and Space Administration (NASA) on November 3, 1973. On March 29, 1974, after twenty-one weeks and a loop around Venus, the little spacecraft approached Mercury, its distant target.

Six days and 124,000 miles (200,000 kilometers) away from Mercury, Mariner 10 began sending back pictures. Scientists were thrilled by what they saw. Because of its proximity to the sun, Mercury looked like a fuzzy ball even through the strongest telescope but through the lens of Mariner's TV camera, Mercury came into sharp focus. For the first time, scientists could see that it is heavily cratered, much like Earth's moon.

After swinging around Mercury, Mariner 10 sent signals from the other side of the planet—130,000 miles (210,000 kilometers) out. Again scientists gained new information as they learned that the back side of the planet is smoother and has fewer craters.

On its closest approach, Mariner 10 came to within 450 miles (725 kilometers) of the little planet. Its 146-day journey enabled scientists to learn more about how Mercury was formed and to map its physical features. Scientific study of the planets in the solar system adds greatly to our understanding of our own planet, Earth.

1. **Recognizing Words in Context**

   Find the word *proximity* in the passage. One definition below is a *synonym* for that word; it means the same or almost the same. One definition is an *antonym;* it has the opposite or nearly opposite meaning. The other has a completely different meaning. Label the definitions S for *synonym*, A for *antonym*, and D for *different*.

   _____ a. distance

   _____ b. nearness

   _____ c. approximation

2. **Distinguishing Fact from Opinion**

   Two of the statements below present *facts,* which can be proved correct. The other statement is an *opinion,* which expresses someone's thoughts or beliefs. Label the statements F for *fact* and O for *opinion.*

   _____ a. Scientists were thrilled by the pictures of Mercury.

   _____ b. Mariner 10 came within 450 miles (725 kilometers) of Mercury.

   _____ c. Scientists used the information from Mariner 10 to map Mercury's physical features.

3. **Keeping Events in Order**

Label the statements below 1, 2, and 3 to show the order in which the events happened.

_____ a. Mariner 10 was launched.

_____ b. Scientists mapped Mercury's physical features.

_____ c. Mariner 10 sent back pictures of Mercury.

4. **Making Correct Inferences**

Two of the statements below are correct *inferences*, or reasonable guesses. They are based on information in the passage. The other statement is an incorrect, or faulty, inference. Label the statements C for *correct* inference and F for *faulty* inference.

_____ a. Scientists could have learned about Mercury through telescopes.

_____ b. Mariner 10 was an important space probe.

_____ c. Learning about Mercury helps scientists in their study of planet Earth.

5. **Understanding Main Ideas**

One of the statements below expresses the main idea of the passage. One statement is too general, or too broad. The other explains only part of the passage; it is too narrow. Label the statements M for *main idea*, B for *too broad*, and N for *too narrow*.

_____ a. Space probes provide useful information about planets.

_____ b. Scientists used the information from the Mariner 10 to map the physical features of Mercury.

_____ c. The Mariner 10 space probe provided new and important information about the features of the planet Mercury.

Correct Answers, Part A _____

Correct Answers, Part B _____

Total Correct Answers _____

44

How Sweet It Is!

Dieters have fewer calories to count and less potential for addiction to sweets when they use sugar substitutes rather than sugar. Some hyperactive children and hypertensive adults can better control themselves when they eat desserts and drink beverages containing artificial sweeteners. For those with diabetes and other medical problems, artificial sweeteners may be preferred to sugar. Some people, however, experience unpleasant reactions to some artificial sweeteners. Artificial sweeteners, which lack food value, are not metabolized by the body and are excreted unchanged.

Saccharin, used in toothpaste, mouthwash, and sugarless gum, was discovered by chemists in 1879 and is from 200 to 700 times sweeter than sucrose (table sugar). Although it has been widely used in dietetic foods and drugs, the Food and Drug Administration (FDA) tried to ban it as an additive in 1977.

Another sweetener, cyclamate, was discovered in 1937, first marketed in 1949, and banned by the FDA as potentially harmful in 1970. Some 30 times sweeter than sugar, it was the artificial sweetener that spawned the diet soft drink industry. A more useful product, aspartame, was discovered accidentally by a drug researcher in 1965, and this sweetener has been marketed under the brand names NutraSweet and Equal since 1983. Although its components occur naturally in foods, aspartame itself must be manufactured. NutraSweet has been a popular ingredient in nearly 3,000 products including diet soft drinks, beverage mixes, puddings, breakfast cereals, and chewing gum. In the late 1980s, the FDA further approved its use in yogurt, fruit-juice and flavored-milk beverages, and ready-to-serve desserts. It is about 200 times sweeter than sugar and can be used in microwave recipes. Many recipes for baked goods, candies, and other products have been modified to allow substitution of aspartame for sugar.

Like aspartame, acesulfame-K is 200 times sweeter than sugar. It has been sold in more than 25 countries since 1983 and, approved by the FDA in 1988, is marketed under the brand names Sunette and Sweet One in the United States. It is stable enough to be substituted for sugar in cooked and baked goods.

Two additional sugar substitutes are mannitol and sorbitol. Mannitol, a white, crystalline substance, is used in gum, candies, and other foods. Sorbitol, because it is absorbed very slowly from the intestine into the bloodstream, can be tolerated by most diabetics. It is used to make gum, candies, and jams and is 60 percent as sweet as sucrose.

Reading Time _____

Recalling Facts

1. The letters FDA stand for
   - ❑ a. Federal Diet Association.
   - ❑ b. Food and Drug Administration.
   - ❑ c. Food Department Agency.

2. The artificial sweetener banned in 1970 is
   - ❑ a. saccharin.
   - ❑ b. cyclamate.
   - ❑ c. sucrose.

3. A disadvantage of artificial sweeteners is that they
   - ❑ a. lack food value.
   - ❑ b. are absorbed slowly into the bloodstream.
   - ❑ c. cannot be tolerated by most diabetics.

4. Aspartame is more useful than cyclamate because it
   - ❑ a. has been approved for use in many foods.
   - ❑ b. must be manufactured.
   - ❑ c. is 200 times sweeter than sugar.

5. Sugar substitutes benefit
   - ❑ a. everyone.
   - ❑ b. hypertensive adults.
   - ❑ c. underactive children.

Understanding Ideas

6. If sorbitol is being substituted for sugar in a recipe,
   - ❑ a. more sorbitol should be used.
   - ❑ b. less sorbitol should be used.
   - ❑ c. the same amount of sorbitol should be used.

7. If aspartame is being substituted for sugar in a recipe,
   - ❑ a. more aspartame should be used.
   - ❑ b. less aspartame should be used.
   - ❑ c. the same amount of aspartame should be used.

8. Potential banning of some sugar substitutes by the FDA suggests that
   - ❑ a. the FDA is overreacting to potential problems.
   - ❑ b. there is reason to take care when using some sugar substitutes.
   - ❑ c. all sugar substitutes should be avoided.

9. Regarding the use of sugar substitutes, the article implies that
   - ❑ a. sugar substitutes are better than sugar.
   - ❑ b. substitutes are not for everyone.
   - ❑ c. only diabetics should use sugar substitutes.

10. There is much research into sugar substitutes, which suggests that
    - ❑ a. sugar is a dangerous substance.
    - ❑ b. scientists should devote more time to this kind of research.
    - ❑ c. there is a need for a safe, tasty sugar substitute.

9 B   Tempest in a Sugar Bowl

Aspartame, a sugar substitute, which is better known by its brand name, NutraSweet, had been on the market about ten years when researchers reported a frightening possibility. They were seeing more and more brain cancer in certain patients, and they wondered aloud if aspartame, which was being used in many different low-calorie products, was the cause or a contributing factor in brain cancer.

The researchers' report hit the headlines, and news programs picked up the story, spreading it around the country. The reports led to concerns about the product's safety, warnings that the sweetener had been approved too quickly, and calls for aspartame to be banned from the marketplace.

Other researchers soon countered the first researchers' allegations. From their studies, they were able to present records that showed that the cancer rate had been rising before aspartame was introduced to the market. Besides, the researchers pointed out, most of the individuals who had developed brain cancer were not users of products that contained aspartame. They could show, moreover, that while the use of aspartame had risen, the cancer rate had actually dropped. Aspartame was proclaimed safe for consumer use and continues to be used by many people who cannot tolerate natural sweeteners.

---

1. **Recognizing Words in Context**

   Find the word *allegations* in the passage. One definition below is a *synonym* for that word; it means the same or almost the same. One definition is an *antonym*; it has the opposite or nearly opposite meaning. The other has a completely different meaning. Label the definitions S for *synonym*, A for *antonym*, and D for *different*.

   _____ a. denials

   _____ b. alliances

   _____ c. claims

2. **Distinguishing Fact from Opinion**

   Two of the statements below present *facts*, which can be proved correct. The other statement is an *opinion*, which expresses someone's thoughts or beliefs. Label the statements F for *fact* and O for *opinion*.

   _____ a. Researchers reported that aspartame might cause brain cancer.

   _____ b. Aspartame was approved too quickly.

   _____ c. Aspartame was declared safe.

3. Keeping Events in Order

Label the statements below 1, 2, and 3 to show the order in which the events happened.

_____ a. News programs and newspapers spread the word that aspartame caused cancer.

_____ b. Researchers announced that aspartame might be unsafe.

_____ c. Researchers proved that the cancer rate had fallen as aspartame use rose.

4. Making Correct Inferences

Two of the statements below are correct *inferences,* or reasonable guesses. They are based on information in the passage. The other statement is an incorrect, or faulty, inference. Label the statements C for *correct* inference and F for *faulty* inference.

_____ a. Research findings are not necessarily true.

_____ b. All products using artificial sweeteners are safe.

_____ c. Aspartame is probably safe.

5. Understanding Main Ideas

One of the statements below expresses the main idea of the passage. One statement is too general, or too broad. The other explains only part of the passage; it is too narrow. Label the statements M for *main idea,* B for *too broad,* and N for *too narrow.*

_____ a. Problems can develop with artificial sweeteners.

_____ b. Aspartame, a sweetener, was believed to be a cause of brain cancer.

_____ c. Aspartame, although once questioned by researchers, is now considered safe to use.

Correct Answers, Part A _____

Correct Answers, Part B _____

Total Correct Answers _____

The Pursuit of Leisure

What is leisure, and must it always be used wisely and well? Different people in different times have defined leisure in different ways. The ancient Greek philosophers, for example, regarded leisure as the labor of the mind, putting to use all one had learned—languages, mathematics, science, music, and the arts—to expand an individual's intellectual horizons and thereby make the person a better citizen. The goal of leisure was to become an educated individual, a goal that one could not attain until well into adulthood. This understanding of leisure is in stark contrast to the late twentieth-century view that regards leisure as time for recreation and for fun.

Today leisure is often regarded as time left over after caring for the needs of existence, such as eating and sleeping, and for subsistence, such as work or education. This leftover time is to be used as each individual chooses. Studies suggest that the average adult spends about 80 to 85 hours weekly for existence and about 35 to 40 hours for subsistence, leaving about 40 to 50 hours of leisure time.

Some people view leisure simply as recreation, an opportunity to engage in sports, hobbies, and other pleasurable activities. Others view leisure as an attitude or frame of mind. Many people consider leisure the main objective of life and work merely as a means to that end. Recent writers have defined leisure as a state of being free, an attitude of mind and condition of soul that helps in experiencing the reality of the world. Still another view defines leisure as a function of social class.

Down through the ages there has always been a leisure class—kings, rulers, and aristocracy—that did not work but lived a life totally supported by slaves, subjects, and servants. People in this class devoted their entire lives to activities that were personally satisfying and convenient. No matter how leisure is defined, the time for it has increased for most people in most cultures. In the United States, for example, the workweek has gradually decreased from six days of 12 hours each to an average of about 34 hours when vacations, holidays, and leaves for illness are considered. Flexible working hours, four-day workweeks, personal leaves, and longer vacations have all allowed more time away from jobs and therefore more time for leisure. The need to use leisure wisely, therefore, is becoming increasingly important.

Reading Time _____

Recalling Facts

1. Early Greeks viewed leisure as a time to pursue
   - ❏ a. recreation.
   - ❏ b. business.
   - ❏ c. education.

2. The weekly leisure time enjoyed by the average American adult is about
   - ❏ a. 30 to 40 hours.
   - ❏ b. 40 to 50 hours.
   - ❏ c. 50 to 60 hours.

3. Recent writers have defined leisure as a
   - ❏ a. means to an end.
   - ❏ b. waste of time.
   - ❏ c. state of mind.

4. Throughout the ages, leisure classes
   - ❏ a. did not work.
   - ❏ b. worked only for the government.
   - ❏ c. worked to obtain riches.

5. In the United States, the workweek has
   - ❏ a. stayed about the same.
   - ❏ b. increased.
   - ❏ c. been reduced.

Understanding Ideas

6. The article suggests that members of the leisure class
   - ❏ a. were bored with their way of life.
   - ❏ b. depended on the existence of the working class.
   - ❏ c. were poorly educated.

7. It is likely that the concept of flexible working hours
   - ❏ a. slows productivity.
   - ❏ b. creates more work for employees.
   - ❏ c. is popular with workers.

8. You can conclude that most people would prefer
   - ❏ a. the same amount of leisure time.
   - ❏ b. more leisure time.
   - ❏ c. less leisure time.

9. Shorter workweeks suggest that
   - ❏ a. people are getting lazier.
   - ❏ b. the social class of workers is changing.
   - ❏ c. leisure time is recognized as being increasingly important.

10. Those who view leisure as an attitude of mind probably regard work as
    - ❏ a. a necessary evil.
    - ❏ b. the main objective of life.
    - ❏ c. part of reality.

"Listen to this, Dave," Odetta Washington said to her husband one
Saturday. She read aloud from the local newspaper that she was holding:
"'Studies suggest that the average adult has 40 to 50 hours of leisure time a
week.' Can you imagine that—40 to 50 hours? What world are the
researchers living in? Certainly they're not living in mine!" She tossed the
paper onto the table and picked up her car keys. "Jameel, Latisha, come
now or we'll be late."

Odetta took Latisha to the rink for her figure skating lesson; then she
headed for the soccer field with Jameel, who had practice. After letting
Jameel out of the car, she hurried through her morning errands: grocery
shopping, picking up dry cleaning, going to the bank. Then it was time to
pick up Latisha at the skating rink. "Don't forget, Mom, I've got to be at
Liz's birthday party at three," Latisha reminded her.

While everyone was gone, Dave had begun his list of chores. He had
taken the storm windows out of the basement, cleaned them, and was
installing them. He was putting the last window in place when Odetta
arrived home with Latisha. As they unloaded the groceries, Odetta called to
Dave, "Enjoying your leisure time, Dave?"

"Just as much as you are!" he answered.

1. **Recognizing Words in Context**

Find the word *headed* in the passage.
One definition below is a *synonym* for
that word; it means the same or
almost the same thing. One definition
is an *antonym;* it has the opposite or
nearly opposite meaning. The other
has a completely different meaning.
Label the definitions S for *synonym,* A
for *antonym,* and D for *different.*

_____ a. led

_____ b. proceeded

_____ c. returned

2. **Distinguishing Fact from Opinion**

Two of the statements below present
facts, which can be proved correct.
The other statement is an *opinion,*
which expresses someone's thoughts
or beliefs. Label the statements F for
fact and O for *opinion.*

_____ a. The people in the study
were not living in the same
world as Odetta and her
family.

_____ b. A study claimed that adults
had 40 to 50 hours of
leisure time a week.

_____ c. Odetta drove Latisha to the
skating rink and Jameel to
the soccer field.

3. Keeping Events in Order

Two of the statements below describe events that happened at the same time. The other statement describes an event that happened before or after those events. Label them S for *same time*, B for *before*, and A for *after*.

_____ a. Odetta, Latisha, and Jameel were out of the house.

_____ b. Odetta read to Dave a newspaper article about leisure time.

_____ c. Dave began working on his list of chores.

4. Making Correct Inferences

Two of the statements below are correct *inferences*, or reasonable guesses. They are based on information in the passage. The other statement is an incorrect, or faulty, inference. Label the statements C for *correct* inference and F for *faulty* inference.

_____ a. Odetta and Dave had no leisure time at all.

_____ b. Odetta spent a lot of time driving her children places.

_____ c. Their family and household chores kept Dave and Odetta very busy.

5. Understanding Main Ideas

One of the statements below expresses the main idea of the passage. One statement is too general, or too broad. The other explains only part of the passage; it is too narrow. Label the statements M for *main idea*, B for *too broad*, and N for *too narrow*.

_____ a. Dave got the storm windows out of the basement, cleaned them, and began installing them.

_____ b. Leisure time is time left over after caring for the needs of existence and subsistence.

_____ c. Contrary to an article stating that adults have 40 to 50 hours of leisure time a week, Odetta and Dave Washington have little real leisure time.

Correct Answers, Part A _____

Correct Answers, Part B _____

Total Correct Answers _____

The Grand Jury

Grand juries are called "grand" because of their size, not because of their function. Grand juries have from 12 to 23 members. The purpose of the grand jury is to inquire whether or not a crime has been committed. A grand jury does not decide upon the issue of guilt or innocence of a suspect; it simply hears testimony and looks at evidence from any number of sources to decide if someone should be indicted for an offense.

Although grand juries are part of the court system, they are not presided over by a judge. The chief officer is a prosecutor from a federal, state, or local jurisdiction, depending on the nature of the offense being investigated. In their proceedings and deliberations, grand juries have far more leeway than do trial juries. Their inquiries may, in fact, become inquisitions because the normal protections afforded the person being questioned (such as the right to the presence of a lawyer) are not allowed. Refusal to answer questions at a grand jury hearing may lead to the imposition of jail sentences for contempt of court.

Grand jury proceedings are informal and secret, although the veil of secrecy may be lifted by the court if it feels the interests of justice will be served. Any unauthorized disclosure of grand jury proceedings is itself an indictable offense in some jurisdictions. If the jury decides, on the basis of testimony and evidence, that a crime has been committed, it presents a bill of indictment. The next step in the justice system is trial in a criminal court.

While grand juries continue to function as part of the court system, particularly on the federal level in the United States, they have come under criticism. Because the rights that witnesses have in court trials are not present in grand jury hearings, many people believe that the hearings seem to deny those protections that are guaranteed by the United States Constitution. Prosecutors have sometimes used grand juries for political ends, manipulating them for personal goals or to serve the interests of a particular political party. Occasionally, details of grand jury hearings are "leaked" to the media. This disclosure often results in widespread (and often unfavorable) publicity for some individual, even when no indictment has been handed down. In some parts of the United States, grand juries are bypassed completely by allowing prosecutions to be initiated directly by elected or appointed prosecutors.

Reading Time _____

Recalling Facts

1. The size of a grand jury may be up to
   - ❏ a. 12 members.
   - ❏ b. 15 members.
   - ❏ c. 23 members.

2. The purpose of a grand jury is to
   - ❏ a. inquire whether a crime has been committed.
   - ❏ b. declare innocence or guilt.
   - ❏ c. determine jail sentences.

3. Grand jury proceedings are
   - ❏ a. open to the public.
   - ❏ b. informal and secret.
   - ❏ c. formal proceedings.

4. Grand jury indictments
   - ❏ a. follow hearings in civil cases.
   - ❏ b. precede criminal court trials.
   - ❏ c. follow criminal court trials.

5. In the United States, grand juries function
   - ❏ a. outside the court system.
   - ❏ b. only on the federal level.
   - ❏ c. as part of the court system.

Understanding Ideas

6. It is likely that suspects in grand jury hearings
   - ❏ a. are usually found guilty in criminal court.
   - ❏ b. are not always indicted.
   - ❏ c. have committed a crime.

7. From the article, you can conclude that juries that determine guilt and innocence
   - ❏ a. have the same function as grand juries.
   - ❏ b. are open to the public.
   - ❏ c. have more members than grand juries.

8. The article suggests that grand juries
   - ❏ a. are an essential part of the court system.
   - ❏ b. may overstep their bounds.
   - ❏ c. serve only to deny the rights of the people.

9. Most likely grand jury hearings have been able to be manipulated because
   - ❏ a. the proceedings are secret.
   - ❏ b. there is no judge.
   - ❏ c. the laws of government do not apply.

10. Grand juries have come under criticism, which suggests that
    - ❏ a. they will most likely be eliminated.
    - ❏ b. there is growing concern for people's rights.
    - ❏ c. the proceedings will be held in public in the future.

Joy read the card in her hands carefully, and a frown began to form on her face. "I've been called for jury duty, starting in two weeks," Joy said as she handed her husband, Lou, the card.

Lou replied, "Maybe you'll have to serve on a jury panel and maybe you won't. Unless you are chosen as a jury member for a big case—which is unlikely—in this state, you have to serve on jury duty usually for only one week. After a week, you get dismissed, and that's it until the next time you're called to serve."

"I've been called for grand jury duty, not petit jury," Joy explained.

"That's different," Lou said. "You may have to serve 30 days if you are selected as a grand jury member!"

"I suppose that it's an honor to serve," Joy said, "but I don't think my boss is going to be happy about this. And we really can't afford to lose my income."

"You don't have to worry about your boss's reaction," said Lou. "Your company isn't allowed to fire you because of jury duty—that's the law. And you get paid for jury duty."

"The pay won't be enough to offset what I'll lose when my pay is docked for the hours I don't work." She shook her head worriedly.

Lou consoled Joy as he reminded her, "It's your civic duty to serve. Everything will work out fine."

1. Recognizing Words in Context

Find the word *fire* in the passage. One definition below is a *synonym* for that word; it means the same or almost the same. One definition is an *antonym*; it has the opposite or nearly opposite meaning. The other has a completely different meaning. Label the definitions S for *synonym*, A for *antonym*, and D for *different*.

_____ a. blaze

_____ b. hire

_____ c. dismiss

2. Distinguishing Fact from Opinion

Two of the statements below present *facts*, which can be proved correct. The other statement is an *opinion*, which expresses someone's thoughts or beliefs. Label the statements F for *fact* and O for *opinion*.

_____ a. It is an honor to serve on the grand jury.

_____ b. Grand jurors may have to serve for 30 days.

_____ c. A person's employer cannot fire a person for being absent because of jury duty.

3. Keeping Events in Order

Two of the statements below describe events that happened at the same time. The other statement describes an event that happened before or after those events. Label them S for *same time,* B for *before,* and A for *after.*

_____ a. Joy held a card in her hands and read it.

_____ b. Joy explained she had been called to serve on the grand jury.

_____ c. Joy was frowning.

4. Making Correct Inferences

Two of the statements below are correct *inferences,* or reasonable guesses. They are based on information in the passage. The other statement is an incorrect, or faulty, inference. Label the statements C for *correct* inference and F for *faulty* inference.

_____ a. Joy would not want to serve on the grand jury under any circumstances.

_____ b. Potential jurors are notified of their selection by mail.

_____ c. Joy's serving on the grand jury could create a financial hardship for Joy and Lou.

5. Understanding Main Ideas

One of the statements below expresses the main idea of the passage. One statement is too general, or too broad. The other explains only part of the passage; it is too narrow. Label the statements M for *main idea,* B for *too broad,* and N for *too narrow.*

_____ a. When Joy is called for grand jury duty, her husband assures her that everything will be fine.

_____ b. Citizens serve on the grand jury.

_____ c. As a grand juror, Joy would have to serve for 30 days.

Correct Answers, Part A _____

Correct Answers, Part B _____

Total Correct Answers _____

The History of Taxes

Tax history for more than 2,500 years has focused on two significant issues: who pays and what is taxed. For most of human history, taxes were paid by the poor peasants, enslaved people, colonists, or conquered peoples to support the government and the wealthy classes. Taxation as the responsibility of free citizens is a modern concept that originated with the emergence of constitutional governments first in England and later in the United States and Western Europe.

In the ancient world until the end of the western Roman Empire in about A.D. 476, governments owned so much of the wealth that taxes were not heavily relied on as sources of revenue. Income from mines, tributes from ruled peoples, and gifts often required from wealthy citizens made up the greatest portion of a government's income. In the time of Julius Caesar in the first century B.C., Rome instituted a 1 percent sales tax, and in the Roman provinces, land was often subject to taxation.

Taxes had little place in the rural feudal system of the Middle Ages. Kings and nobles made their livings from land held directly or through payments from the people who worked the land. As the social system of the Middle Ages broke up, land became the primary source of wealth and taxation. In France, a tax was levied on estimated farm income, while in England, land taxes were first based on area but later on annual rental value. In British North America, the English land tax system was broadened into a property tax with a base that included land, houses, personal property, and the earning capacity of the individuals who owned the land.

Rebellion against oppressive tax systems played a major role in both the American and French revolutions. The subsequent establishment of representative democracies along with the modern ideal of social justice helped bring about the reform of tax systems.

The emergence of the modern economic system with its varied sources of income and wealth also led to the more uniform system of taxing income directly. The first modern income tax was adopted in England. In the United States, an income tax was used by the Union as a temporary measure during the Civil War. In 1894 the income tax was again enacted, but it was later declared unconstitutional. As a result, the Sixteenth Amendment to the Constitution, establishing a national income tax, was adopted in 1913.

Reading Time _____

Recalling Facts

1. The two significant issues of tax history have been who pays and
   - ❏ a. what is taxed.
   - ❏ b. whether taxation is legal.
   - ❏ c. how to collect taxes.

2. In the time of Julius Caesar, Rome instituted
   - ❏ a. a 1 percent sales tax.
   - ❏ b. a land tax.
   - ❏ c. inheritance taxes.

3. During the Middle Ages, taxes
   - ❏ a. were paid by nobles.
   - ❏ b. were the source of income in the feudal system.
   - ❏ c. had little place in the feudal system.

4. After the Middle Ages, taxes were typically levied on those who
   - ❏ a. owned land.
   - ❏ b. could least afford to pay.
   - ❏ c. worked in industry.

5. The first modern income tax was adopted in
   - ❏ a. the United States.
   - ❏ b. France.
   - ❏ c. England.

Understanding Ideas

6. Taxes as a source of revenue is
   - ❏ a. a new concept.
   - ❏ b. an age-old concept.
   - ❏ c. an unconstitutional concept.

7. Unlike past taxation systems, today's system
   - ❏ a. relies on payment from free citizens.
   - ❏ b. assesses taxes haphazardly.
   - ❏ c. places most of the tax burden on the poor.

8. Taxation on land in the past suggests that land ownership was
   - ❏ a. an insignificant source of wealth.
   - ❏ b. a major source of wealth.
   - ❏ c. a minor source of wealth.

9. You can conclude from the article that historically, taxation systems were
   - ❏ a. considered fair by most people.
   - ❏ b. ignored by most people.
   - ❏ c. considered oppressive by most people.

10. It is likely that the modern income tax system
    - ❏ a. is subject to reform.
    - ❏ b. will most likely be declared unconstitutional.
    - ❏ c. is here to stay.

12 B   The Boston Tea Party

"No taxation without representation!" was the cry throughout the
American colonies in the 1770s. The colonists had no representatives in the
British Parliament, and they were determined not to pay taxes to a government in which they had no voice. Rebellion was in the air. The situation
worsened in May 1773 when Parliament passed the Tea Act, which gave the
British East India Company the right to sell its tea in the colonies without
payment of duty charges. Colonial tea merchants objected bitterly because
the East India Company could now undersell them.

On the night of December 16, 1773, the Sons of Liberty—rebels led by
Samuel Adams—took action. Some disguised themselves as Mohawks in war
paint and blankets. Others wore rags with lampblack smeared on their faces.
The rebels divided into three groups of 50 each and boarded three tea ships
in Boston Harbor. They axed open 342 chests of tea and dumped it into
the harbor "to steep." This act became known as the Boston Tea Party.

A song titled "Revolutionary Tea" that was written at the time recounts
the sauciness of an American daughter to her English mother. It ends with
this refrain:

"Your tea you may have when 'tis steeped enough
But never a tax from me,
But never a tax from me."

1. Recognizing Words in Context

Find the word *boarded* in the passage.
One definition below is a *synonym* for
that word; it means the same or
almost the same. One definition is an
antonym; it has the opposite or nearly
opposite meaning. The other has a
completely different meaning. Label
the definitions S for *synonym*, A for
antonym, and D for *different*.

_____ a. left

_____ b. covered

_____ c. got on

2. Distinguishing Fact from Opinion

Two of the statements below present
facts, which can be proved correct.
The other statement is an *opinion*,
which expresses someone's thoughts
or beliefs. Label the statements F for
fact and O for *opinion*.

_____ a. The Tea Act gave the East
India Company the right to
sell tea free of duty charges.

_____ b. The Sons of Liberty threw
342 chests of tea into
Boston Harbor.

_____ c. The colonists were entitled
to representation in
Parliament.

3. Keeping Events in Order

Label the statements below 1, 2, and 3 to show the order in which the events happened.

_____ a. The Sons of Liberty disguised themselves and boarded three tea ships in Boston Harbor.

_____ b. Parliament passed the Tea Act.

_____ c. Tea merchants were angry because the East India Company could undersell them.

4. Making Correct Inferences

Two of the statements below are correct *inferences,* or reasonable guesses. They are based on information in the passage. The other statement is an incorrect, or faulty, inference. Label the statements C for *correct* inference and F for *faulty* inference.

_____ a. Colonial tea merchants had to pay duty charges on the tea they sold.

_____ b. All of the tea in the colonies was dumped during the Boston Tea Party.

_____ c. The daughter in the song was the American colonies, and the mother was England.

5. Understanding Main Ideas

One of the statements below expresses the main idea of the passage. One statement is too general, or too broad. The other explains only part of the passage; it is too narrow. Label the statements M for *main idea,* B for *too broad,* and N for *too narrow.*

_____ a. A combination of new taxes and restrictive laws led American colonists to rebel against the British.

_____ b. In an act known as the Boston Tea Party, American colonists dumped 342 cases of tea into Boston Harbor in 1773.

_____ c. In 1773 Parliament passed the Tea Act.

Correct Answers, Part A _____

Correct Answers, Part B _____

Total Correct Answers _____

I Love a Parade

Holidays, athletic contests, religious observances, and other festivities are often celebrated with pageants or parades. The college football bowl games played in the United States every New Year's Day are preceded by parades. The parade before the Orange Bowl game in Miami, Florida, takes place on the evening of December 31, while the Cotton Bowl parade in Dallas, Texas, and the Tournament of Roses parade in Pasadena, California, are held on January 1.

A *parade,* by definition, is a procession of people and perhaps floats, bands, vehicles, and animals. A *pageant,* however, can be a series of staged dramatic performances, such as re-creations of battles or colorful parades with floats organized around some unifying theme. In Great Britain, the coronation of Elizabeth II in 1953 was carried out with great pageantry. One of the most elaborate pageants ever staged was the four-day extravaganza celebrating the 100th birthday of the Statue of Liberty in 1986.

Pageants have been held throughout the ages. For example, during the Middle Ages, tournaments were held in which mock battles were fought between knights. Closely related to these jousts were displays of horse riding ability such as those held at the Spanish Riding School in Vienna, Austria. Bullfights in Spain begin with colorful ceremonies in which all participants enter the ring, many on horseback; and today's circus is also a form of pageant.

Pageantry and parades originated as religious rituals among very ancient peoples. Early peoples held dances or processions to frighten away evil spirits or to demonstrate military strength. The ancient Chinese made paper and wooden images of dragon gods and carried them through the streets to make it rain. Traditional dragon parades are still part of Chinese New Year celebrations.

One of the best-known annual celebrations with religious roots is the Mardi Gras. It has long been a popular festival time celebrated in Roman Catholic countries before the solemn season of Lent begins. In the United States, the Mardi Gras festivities in New Orleans, Louisiana, featuring masked balls and parades, are a major tourist attraction. The celebration ends on Shrove Tuesday, the day before Ash Wednesday, the first day of Lent. In parts of Germany, especially around Cologne, the pre-Lenten celebration begins in November. The festivities begin at the eleventh hour of the eleventh day of the eleventh month, but the height of the merrymaking does not get under way until the Thursday before Lent.

Reading Time _____

Recalling Facts

1. Pageants and parades originated
   - ❏ a. to ward off evil spirits.
   - ❏ b. as religious rituals.
   - ❏ c. as athletic ceremonies.

2. Mardi Gras is an annual celebration preceding
   - ❏ a. college bowl football games.
   - ❏ b. Chinese New Year.
   - ❏ c. Lent.

3. A parade is defined as people
   - ❏ a. performing in plays.
   - ❏ b. taking part in tournaments.
   - ❏ c. in procession.

4. Staged dramatic performances are examples of
   - ❏ a. parades.
   - ❏ b. pageants.
   - ❏ c. tournaments.

5. The last day of Mardi Gras is
   - ❏ a. Shrove Tuesday.
   - ❏ b. Ash Wednesday.
   - ❏ c. New Year's Day.

Understanding Ideas

6. The article wants you to understand that parades
   - ❏ a. are joyous celebrations.
   - ❏ b. are religious services.
   - ❏ c. usually revolve around the seasons.

7. You can conclude from the article that parades
   - ❏ a. have lost their appeal.
   - ❏ b. are as popular as ever.
   - ❏ c. are becoming less elaborate than they once were.

8. The reenactment of the Battle of Lexington would be considered
   - ❏ a. a religious observance.
   - ❏ b. pageantry.
   - ❏ c. a parade.

9. Parades precede college football games played in the United States every New Year's Day, which suggests that
   - ❏ a. Americans are big football fans.
   - ❏ b. these parades are religious in nature.
   - ❏ c. parades have become a ritual in the United States.

10. You can conclude from the article that parades and pageantry
    - ❏ a. are popular mostly in the United States.
    - ❏ b. have universal appeal.
    - ❏ c. are popular mostly in Europe.

13 B America's Favorite Parade

Every year on the night before Thanksgiving, workers bring huge balloons, 50 to 80 feet (15 to 25 meters) long, from storage and spread them on the ground. The workers attach helium hoses to nozzles in the balloons, and the balloons begin to take shape. "There's Spider Man!" "There's Bugs Bunny!" The inflation of the balloons is just one indication that the annual Macy's Thanksgiving Day Parade will soon be under way in New York City.

The Macy's parade began in 1924 with real animals, but rubber balloons filled with air replaced the live animals in 1927. Balloons filled with helium came next; after the parade was over, the handlers released the balloons. In 1929, Macy's offered gift certificates to anyone who found and returned a balloon.

During World War II, the parade was canceled, and the rubber was donated to the war effort. Since then, the parade has never missed a year—rain, snow, or shine—but not without mishap. In 1957, the Popeye balloon collected rainwater by the hatful, which was periodically dumped on the onlookers. In 1989, a storm coated the balloons with ice, and when sharp pieces of ice punctured Superman's leg, the balloon collapsed in a tangle of rope.

Whatever happens, America's favorite parade goes on. As TV cameras roll, hundreds of handlers, dozens of bands, floats, performers, and balloons make their way down Broadway to the delight of millions of viewers—young and old.

1. **Recognizing Words in Context**

   Find the word *donated* in the passage. One definition below is a *synonym* for that word; it means the same or almost the same. One definition is an *antonym;* it has the opposite or nearly opposite meaning. The other has a completely different meaning. Label the definitions S for *synonym,* A for *antonym,* and D for *different.*

   _____ a. controlled

   _____ b. given

   _____ c. withheld

2. **Distinguishing Fact from Opinion**

   Two of the statements below present *facts,* which can be proved correct. The other statement is an *opinion,* which expresses someone's thoughts or beliefs. Label the statements F for *fact* and O for *opinion.*

   _____ a. The Macy's parade began in 1924.

   _____ b. Macy's parade is America's favorite.

   _____ c. The first parade balloons were filled with air.

3. **Keeping Events in Order**

   Label the statements below 1, 2, and 3 to show the order in which the events happened.

   _____ a. An ice storm caused the Superman balloon to collapse.

   _____ b. People got gift certificates for returning balloons.

   _____ c. The Macy's parade was canceled during World War II.

4. **Making Correct Inferences**

   Two of the statements below are correct *inferences*, or reasonable guesses. They are based on information in the passage. The other statement is an incorrect, or faulty, inference. Label the statements C for *correct* inference and F for *faulty* inference.

   _____ a. The Macy's parade always goes off without a hitch.

   _____ b. Weather is often a problem for the Macy's parade.

   _____ c. Parade practices have changed over the years.

5. **Understanding Main Ideas**

   One of the statements below expresses the main idea of the passage. One statement is too general, or too broad. The other explains only part of the passage; it is too narrow. Label the statements M for *main idea*, B for *too broad*, and N for *too narrow*.

   _____ a. The Macy's parade has a long and event-filled history.

   _____ b. Many people participate in parades.

   _____ c. Snow and rain sometimes disrupt the Macy's parade, but it continues on its way.

Correct Answers, Part A _____

Correct Answers, Part B _____

Total Correct Answers _____

Can people control their own evolution in order to achieve a population free of physical and mental defects? For more than 100 years, individuals who support eugenics, the study of human change by genetic means, have answered "yes."

The word *eugenics* comes from a Greek word that means "wellborn." Supporters of eugenics seek to change the human race through artificial selection. This refers to the controlled breeding of people who have certain physical characteristics or mental abilities. Eugenics is based on the science of genetics, the science that studies how genes are structured and passed on through generations. Eugenics also involves the use of information obtained from other areas of knowledge. Psychology, the study of personality; medicine, as it relates to the genetic factors of certain diseases and conditions; sociology, the study of group interaction; and demography, the statistical study of human populations, are some of the disciplines upon which eugenic theories are based.

Ideas about improving animal and plant stocks have existed since ancient times. Many animals, especially dogs and horses, have been bred to improve specific characteristics. Trees and other plants have also been bred to obtain hardier and more productive strains. Thoughts about improving human beings by such means existed in ancient times. The famous Greek philosopher Plato discussed such possibilities in his *The Republic*.

Current interest in eugenics involves studying the nature and causes of genetic defects, the ways in which psychological traits are determined, and the relationship between environmental factors and heredity. Scientists believe that today the number of people who are carrying defective genes is increasing. Part of the explanation for this increase is that more people are being exposed to damaging radiation, chemicals, and other environmental hazards. Another reason may lie in generations of poor nutrition. Medical advances, however, have made it possible for people with inherited diseases and other deficiencies to live longer and to produce children.

Each year increasing numbers of genetic defects are being defined, the ways in which they are transmitted are better understood, and methods for identifying carriers of such defects are being improved. The controversial field of genetic surgery, in which harmful genes are altered by direct manipulation, is also being studied. An international effort is being made to locate and map all of the genes that make up a human being. This project, when completed, should greatly help efforts to understand genetic makeup and control genetic defects.

Reading Time _____

Recalling Facts

1. The science of genetics studies
   - ❏ a. group interaction.
   - ❏ b. how genes are structured and passed on.
   - ❏ c. the statistics of human population.

2. The word *eugenics* comes from a Greek word meaning
   - ❏ a. "wellborn."
   - ❏ b. "intelligent."
   - ❏ c. "heredity."

3. Changing the human race through artificial selection is a concept of
   - ❏ a. psychology.
   - ❏ b. eugenics.
   - ❏ c. philosophy.

4. Scientists believe that the number of people who are carrying defective genes is
   - ❏ a. staying about the same.
   - ❏ b. decreasing.
   - ❏ c. increasing.

5. In genetic surgery,
   - ❏ a. genes are transferred from one part of the body to another.
   - ❏ b. genes are added to the body.
   - ❏ c. harmful genes are altered by direct manipulation.

Understanding Ideas

6. You can conclude from the article that genetic defects
   - ❏ a. are an avoidable result of modern technology.
   - ❏ b. can be controlled.
   - ❏ c. are worsened by stress.

7. A factor that proponents of the eugenics theory would most likely prefer in people is
   - ❏ a. low level of intelligence.
   - ❏ b. average intelligence.
   - ❏ c. above average intelligence.

8. The concept of controlling genetic defects
   - ❏ a. is a new concept.
   - ❏ b. has been an international concern.
   - ❏ c. attracts more detractors than supporters.

9. As people live longer, the likelihood of defective genes in the population
   - ❏ a. stays the same.
   - ❏ b. decreases.
   - ❏ c. increases.

10. The concept of changing the human race through artificial selection is apt to be
    - ❏ a. a controversial issue.
    - ❏ b. limited to scientific debate.
    - ❏ c. a nonissue.

14   B   Positive Eugenics

Anna carries a "bad gene." Her younger brother had a rare genetic defect that causes mental retardation and physical deformity. Anna loved her brother, but she saw him suffer terribly and die at the age of 12 when his weak lungs failed completely. She dreaded the thought that she might have a child with the same devastating condition.

The genetic defect that killed Anna's brother is carried in the female line. Women with the gene are normal and healthy, but their sons may inherit the condition. Genetic studies showed that Anna and her sisters all carried the faulty gene.

Genetic counselors met with Anna to explain what she faced if she decided to have children. Each child would have a 50 percent chance of inheriting her gene. A boy who inherited it would have the deadly condition, and a girl would be a carrier.

When Anna became pregnant, she immediately had a test to find out the baby's sex. She and her husband were relieved to learn that their baby was a girl. Although Anna's daughter may be a carrier, she is healthy. When she is older, Anna will have her tested to find out if she carries the faulty gene. With luck, she will not.

---

1. **Recognizing Words in Context**

   Find the word *devastating* in the passage. One definition below is a *synonym* for that word; it means the same or almost the same. One definition is an *antonym;* it has the opposite or nearly opposite meaning. The other has a completely different meaning. Label the definitions S for *synonym,* A for *antonym,* and D for *different.*

   _____ a. destroying

   _____ b. ineffective

   _____ c. overwhelming

2. **Distinguishing Fact from Opinion**

   Two of the statements below present *facts,* which can be proved correct. The other statement is an *opinion,* which expresses someone's thoughts or beliefs. Label the statements F for *fact* and O for *opinion.*

   _____ a. Anna and her sisters all carry the faulty gene.

   _____ b. This genetic defect is carried in the female line.

   _____ c. Anna and her husband should not have taken a chance by having a baby.

3. **Keeping Events in Order**

Label the statements below 1, 2, and 3 to show the order in which the events happened.

_____ a. Anna's brother died of a genetic disease.

_____ b. Anna had a healthy baby girl.

_____ c. Anna talks with counselors about having a baby.

4. **Making Correct Inferences**

Two of the statements below are correct *inferences*, or reasonable guesses. They are based on information in the passage. The other statement is an incorrect, or faulty, inference. Label the statements C for *correct* inference and F for *faulty* inference.

_____ a. Genetic counselors help people evaluate genetic risks.

_____ b. Any son of Anna's would have the genetic defect.

_____ c. Genetic counseling helped Anna decide to have a child.

5. **Understanding Main Ideas**

One of the statements below expresses the main idea of the passage. One statement is too general, or too broad. The other explains only part of the passage; it is too narrow. Label the statements M for *main idea*, B for *too broad*, and N for *too narrow*.

_____ a. The science of genetics enables people to know whether they are at risk for genetic defects.

_____ b. Genetic counselors met with Anna to explain what she faced if she decided to have a child.

_____ c. Anna, a woman with a defective gene that can cause a serious condition, had received genetic counseling and later had a healthy child.

Correct Answers, Part A _____

Correct Answers, Part B _____

Total Correct Answers _____

The Constitution of the United States states: "The President, Vice President and all civil Officers of the United States, shall be removed from Office on Impeachment for, and Conviction of, Treason, Bribery, or other high Crimes and Misdemeanors." Impeachment is a legal procedure whereby a public official is indicted for, or accused of, misdeeds he or she is suspected of having committed.

When a government official is implicated in wrongdoing, a legislative body, such as the House of Representatives, conducts hearings to weigh evidence against the accused. If the legislature decides that there is a good case against the accused, it will vote a bill of impeachment. This does not mean that the individual is guilty. However, it does mean that there must be a trial.

At the federal level of government in the United States, the trial is conducted by the Senate after the House of Representatives has voted the bill of impeachment. The Senate, therefore, takes on the role of jury, and it votes, on the basis of the evidence, to acquit or convict the accused. If an official is convicted, the President, according to the Constitution, has no power to pardon him or her.

Because of a popular outcry against officials, impeachment originated in England during the fourteenth century. It was used as a legal means of instituting criminal proceedings against public officials. The Good Parliament of 1376 produced the first recognized cases of impeachment against certain officers who had been associated with the government of King Edward III.

After the mid-fifteenth century, the practice lapsed until the seventeenth century when Parliament revived it as a convenient means of getting rid of unpopular ministers, usually officials who were favorites of the king. However, the use of the impeachment process declined, since it was generally recognized that Parliament had often abused the power.

In the United States, the impeachment process has rarely been employed, but there have been two infamous cases involving it. Andrew Johnson, who succeeded Abraham Lincoln in the presidency, is the only President to have been impeached. At his trial in the Senate, Johnson was acquitted by only one vote. The other case involved President Richard M. Nixon. As a result of the Watergate scandal, the Judiciary Committee of the House of Representatives voted three articles of a bill of impeachment against Nixon in July 1974, but Nixon resigned before impeachment proceedings could begin.

Reading Time _____

Recalling Facts

1. According to the Constitution, an official who is impeached and convicted must be
   - ❏ a. fined.
   - ❏ b. removed from office.
   - ❏ c. jailed.

2. When a bill of impeachment is voted,
   - ❏ a. an individual is declared guilty.
   - ❏ b. the accused is pardoned.
   - ❏ c. there must be a trial.

3. At the federal level of government in the United States, impeachment trials are decided by
   - ❏ a. both houses of Congress.
   - ❏ b. the Senate.
   - ❏ c. the House of Representatives.

4. The only President of the United States to be impeached was
   - ❏ a. Abraham Lincoln.
   - ❏ b. Andrew Johnson.
   - ❏ c. Richard Nixon.

5. The use of impeachment declined in England because
   - ❏ a. the king abolished it.
   - ❏ b. Parliament often abused its power.
   - ❏ c. it wasn't needed.

Understanding Ideas

6. By outlining the impeachment process in the Constitution, its writers
   - ❏ a. misinterpreted the purpose of impeachment.
   - ❏ b. took a negative view of human nature.
   - ❏ c. exhibited prudence.

7. The impeachment process makes the assumption that
   - ❏ a. power breeds corruption.
   - ❏ b. a person is guilty until proven innocent.
   - ❏ c. a person is innocent until proven guilty.

8. The impeachment process can be compared to
   - ❏ a. a jury trial.
   - ❏ b. a political campaign.
   - ❏ c. an athletic contest.

9. You can conclude that if Richard Nixon had not resigned,
   - ❏ a. he would have been declared guilty.
   - ❏ b. he would have undergone impeachment proceedings.
   - ❏ c. there would have been no impeachment proceedings.

10. Andrew Johnson's impeachment and acquittal can be seen as
    - ❏ a. the Senate's failure to enact justice.
    - ❏ b. the failure of the impeachment process.
    - ❏ c. justice in action.

15 B The Case Against Andrew Johnson

Andrew Johnson, the seventeenth President of the United States, is the only President to have been impeached. He had made too many enemies in Congress.

After serving two terms as governor of Tennessee, Andrew Johnson was elected to the U.S. Senate in 1857. When the southern states withdrew from the Union, every southerner in Congress left except one—Andrew Johnson. "I voted against Lincoln," Johnson said. "I spoke against him. . . . But still I love my country." When Lincoln ran for a second term in 1864, Johnson was his vice presidential running mate. After Lincoln's assassination in April 1865, Johnson was sworn in as President.

With the Civil War over, Johnson did not want to take revenge on the southern states for leaving the Union. He made speeches urging moderate treatment of the South, and he also strongly opposed granting former slaves the right to become citizens and vote. Because of Johnson's strong ideas, which differed from those held by many congressional leaders, Congress wanted to get rid of Johnson. There were no lawful grounds for the charges brought against Johnson, but in the Senate trial, 36 out of 54 senators voted to impeach him. Because the law required a two-thirds majority to impeach, Andrew Johnson missed being put out of office by just one vote!

1. **Recognizing Words in Context**

   Find the word *grounds* in the passage. One definition below is a *synonym* for that word; it means the same or almost the same. One definition is an *antonym;* it has the opposite or nearly opposite meaning. The other has a completely different meaning. Label the definitions S for *synonym,* A for *antonym,* and D for *different.*

   _____ a. land

   _____ b. cause

   _____ c. effect

2. **Distinguishing Fact from Opinion**

   Two of the statements below present *facts,* which can be proved correct. The other statement is an *opinion,* which expresses someone's thoughts or beliefs. Label the statements F for *fact* and O for *opinion.*

   _____ a. Andrew Johnson was wrong to oppose citizenship for former slaves.

   _____ b. Andrew Johnson was the only U.S. President to be impeached.

   _____ c. Andrew Johnson was the only southern senator to remain loyal to the Union.

3. **Keeping Events in Order**

Label the statements below 1, 2, and 3 to show the order in which the events happened.

_____ a. Andrew Johnson was President Lincoln's Vice President.

_____ b. Congress wanted to impeach, or get rid of, Andrew Johnson.

_____ c. Andrew Johnson stayed in Congress when other southern senators left.

4. **Making Correct Inferences**

Two of the statements below are correct *inferences*, or reasonable guesses. They are based on information in the passage. The other statement is an incorrect, or faulty, inference. Label the statements C for *correct* inference and F for *faulty* inference.

_____ a. Andrew Johnson was impeached because most members of Congress did not agree with him.

_____ b. Some members of Congress wanted the southern states to be punished for having left the Union.

_____ c. Andrew Johnson would never have become President if Lincoln had not been assassinated.

5. **Understanding Main Ideas**

One of the statements below expresses the main idea of the passage. One statement is too general, or too broad. The other explains only part of the passage; it is too narrow. Label the statements M for *main idea*, B for *too broad*, and N for *too narrow*.

_____ a. Andrew Johnson served as Vice President during Lincoln's second term as President.

_____ b. Andrew Johnson, the only U.S. President to be impeached, was acquitted by only one vote.

_____ c. Impeachment is a legal procedure whereby a public official is accused of and tried for misdeeds.

Correct Answers, Part A _____

Correct Answers, Part B _____

Total Correct Answers _____

　　　Escalators and Moving Sidewalks

Within relatively confined areas such as office buildings, airport terminals, and large ships, the movement of people and freight is usually accomplished by means of elevators, escalators, and moving sidewalks. Elevators, or lifts, carry passengers and freight up and down; escalators are moving staircases from one story of a building to the next; and moving sidewalks carry people horizontally or at a slight incline.

The escalator is a moving staircase in which the steps move as a unit upward or downward at an incline of about 30 degrees. The advantages of the escalator over the elevator are its greater passenger capacity (as many as 6,000 persons per hour on larger types), continuous availability, comparatively small space requirements, and lower operating cost.

The first escalator was an inclined belt invented in 1891 by Jesse W. Reno in the United States. Passengers rode on cleats, or wedge-shaped supports, attached to the belt, which was at an incline of 25 degrees. In the same year, a moving handrail was added, and horizontal steps were added by Charles D. Seeberger later in the 1890s. The Otis Elevator Company acquired both inventions, and the first installations of escalators were at the Paris Exposition of 1900 and in the New York City subway system.

The average distance between the stories in a building is 12 feet (3.7 meters). Because of the 30-degree incline, a story-to-story escalator is about 60 feet (18 meters) long although some are much longer. In the London underground, or subway, stations, some escalators rise four stories. The longest escalator, which is 745 feet (227 meters) long and rises to a height of 377 feet (115 meters), is located in the Ocean Park area of Hong Kong. It can carry 4,000 people an hour in each direction. In some rare cases, escalators are attached to the outside of buildings.

Moving sidewalks, sometimes called travelators or people movers, use the technology originally developed for the escalator to carry people over horizontal levels or at a slight incline. The ramps have either solid or jointed treads or a continuous belt, and their chief use has been in enclosed areas, such as airports, in which people, especially those with carry-on luggage, need to walk relatively long distances in a short time. A number of the world's largest and busiest airports have installed them in their terminals and in tunnels going from one building to another.

Reading Time _____

Recalling Facts

1. Escalators are
   - ❏ a. horizontal ramps.
   - ❏ b. lifts that carry passengers up and down.
   - ❏ c. moving staircases between stories.

2. One advantage of the escalator over the elevator is
   - ❏ a. lower cost.
   - ❏ b. greater safety.
   - ❏ c. infrequent availability.

3. The first escalator was invented
   - ❏ a. before 1900.
   - ❏ b. in the early 1900s.
   - ❏ c. in the 1930s.

4. Escalators were first installed in
   - ❏ a. Hong Kong.
   - ❏ b. Paris and New York City.
   - ❏ c. London.

5. The longest escalator in service is located in
   - ❏ a. Hong Kong.
   - ❏ b. Paris and New York City.
   - ❏ c. London.

Understanding Ideas

6. An escalator would probably be preferable to an elevator
   - ❏ a. where people need to walk long distances.
   - ❏ b. if the budget is unlimited.
   - ❏ c. in a two-story building.

7. It is likely that escalators are attached to the outside of buildings because
   - ❏ a. more people can be transported.
   - ❏ b. space inside the building is limited.
   - ❏ c. the weather is good year-round.

8. You can conclude from the article that the choice of how to move people in confined areas
   - ❏ a. is usually a matter of chance.
   - ❏ b. depends primarily on the amount of space available.
   - ❏ c. depends on a variety of factors.

9. A high-rise building would most likely choose to install
   - ❏ a. an escalator.
   - ❏ b. an elevator.
   - ❏ c. a moving sidewalk.

10. It is likely that before the invention of escalators and elevators,
    - ❏ a. there were few very tall buildings.
    - ❏ b. many tall buildings were built.
    - ❏ c. moving sidewalks were found in most tall buildings.

Down the Up Escalator

Rafe had planned to meet his friends at the mall where they would grab something to eat and then go to the video arcade. Before he could leave the house, however, his mother stopped him, saying, "One of my patients just called, and she's on her way to the hospital to deliver a baby. I can't get a sitter on such short notice, so you have to watch Jaime."

"I guess you'll have to come to the mall with me," Rafe told his younger brother.

At the mall, Rafe and Jaime rode the escalator to the second level, where Rafe and his friends were meeting at the food court. As Rafe stepped off the escalator, he turned around just in time to see Jaime begin walking down the up escalator. "Jaime," Rafe yelled, "Get back here!"

Jaime paid no attention. With people scattering out of his way, Jaime laughed and exclaimed, "This is fun!"

Rafe dashed to the down escalator, reached the first level, and headed for the up escalator. The stairs carried him swiftly toward his brother, whom Rafe grabbed, picked up, and carried off the escalator. "That was a lot of fun, Rafe," Jaime said.

Rafe just grumpily grunted. He couldn't begin to guess what his kid brother would do next, but he promised himself that he wouldn't let Jaime out of his sight for a second.

1. **Recognizing Words in Context**

   Find the word *dashed* in the passage. One definition below is a *synonym* for that word; it means the same or almost the same. One definition is an *antonym;* it has the opposite or nearly opposite meaning. The other has a completely different meaning. Label the definitions S for *synonym*, A for *antonym*, and D for *different*.

   _____ a. hurried

   _____ b. dawdled

   _____ c. ruined

2. **Distinguishing Fact from Opinion**

   Two of the statements below present *facts*, which can be proved correct. The other statement is an *opinion*, which expresses someone's thoughts or beliefs. Label the statements F for *fact* and O for *opinion*.

   _____ a. Jaime tried to go down the up escalator.

   _____ b. Rafe was meeting friends at the mall.

   _____ c. Going down the up escalator is a fun thing to do.

3. Keeping Events in Order

Two of the statements below describe events that happened at the same time. The other statement describes an event that happened before or after those events. Label them S for *same time,* B for *before,* and A for *after.*

_____ a. Jaime got back onto the up escalator.

_____ b. Rafe carried his brother off the escalator.

_____ c. Jaime said that he had a lot of fun on the escalator.

4. Making Correct Inferences

Two of the statements below are correct *inferences,* or reasonable guesses. They are based on information in the passage. The other statement is an incorrect, or faulty, inference. Label the statements C for *correct* inference and F for *faulty* inference.

_____ a. The boys' mother is a doctor.

_____ b. Rafe was a responsible baby-sitter.

_____ c. Rafe did not like his younger brother.

5. Understanding Main Ideas

One of the statements below expresses the main idea of the passage. One statement is too general, or too broad. The other explains only part of the passage; it is too narrow. Label the statements M for *main idea,* B for *too broad,* and N for *too narrow.*

_____ a. Rafe's mother asked him to take care of Jaime, his younger brother.

_____ b. Rafe's younger brother, Jaime, played a prank on the escalator at the mall.

_____ c. Many malls are on more than one level, with escalators connecting the levels.

Correct Answers, Part A _____

Correct Answers, Part B _____

Total Correct Answers _____

17 A   Mass Production

The manufacture of a product in large numbers and at a low cost, using specialized equipment and a division of labor, is called mass production. The improved standards of living in many industrialized countries over the last two centuries are due largely to mass production.

By dividing a job into several small tasks, each task is performed more efficiently, and productivity increases. Division of labor helps workers perform specialized tasks more effectively. However, this works only when the component parts are interchangeable, or essentially identical. Each part must be produced to close tolerances and meet quality standards.

Mass production can involve single items, such as the making of nuts or bolts, or it may require both production of parts and assembly. Mass production techniques for a complex product were first applied in the high-speed assembly line of the Ford automotive plant in Detroit, Michigan, in 1913. With only minor modifications and different interchangeable parts, successive vehicles were passed along the line.

The heart of an assembly system is the conveyor belt, a moving device (not necessarily a belt) on which the product is assembled. As the belt moves at a set speed, often with short stops, parts are added and various operations are performed. Each task has an allotted time. At various stages along the assembly, it is possible to add components made elsewhere.

Modern mass production is sometimes aided by numerically controlled automatic machining on equipment that performs all machining sequences as determined by a computer program. This may be coupled with computer-aided design in which the parts are designed with the help of a computer.

The handling of parts and their positioning on machines may be performed by a human operator or a robotic arm. Robotic devices are used more and more in a number of industries to perform simple operations, to improve speed and accuracy, and to lessen the chance for worker injury.

Mass production has also led to the increased modularization of components. By developing subassemblies that can be incorporated readily in the final product, the cost of assembly is reduced. One problem being faced by mass production is that workers perform the same task over and over and are unable to identify their contribution to the final product. The scope of the individual is being enlarged to remedy inefficiency caused by boredom or fatigue and to reduce errors introduced by performing the same jobs repetitively.

Reading Time _____

Recalling Facts

1. In mass production, jobs are
   - ❏ a. divided into several small tasks.
   - ❏ b. grouped together by specialty.
   - ❏ c. organized by computer.

2. The first complex products assembled by mass production were
   - ❏ a. motor vehicles.
   - ❏ b. computers.
   - ❏ c. nuts and bolts.

3. In mass production, a product is assembled on
   - ❏ a. a large wheel.
   - ❏ b. a conveyor belt.
   - ❏ c. moving stairs.

4. Each assembly in mass production is performed
   - ❏ a. by robots.
   - ❏ b. by machines.
   - ❏ c. in an allotted time.

5. To reduce worker injury in mass production,
   - ❏ a. assembly lines are slowed down.
   - ❏ b. some components are assembled ahead of time.
   - ❏ c. robots are used instead of humans.

Understanding Ideas

6. It is likely that assembly lines reduce
   - ❏ a. quality standards.
   - ❏ b. efficiency.
   - ❏ c. cost.

7. An advantage of robots over humans in assembly lines is that
   - ❏ a. robots never tire.
   - ❏ b. robots need maintenance.
   - ❏ c. robots can perform the same jobs repetitively.

8. You can conclude that a factor that negatively influences worker efficiency is
   - ❏ a. factory location.
   - ❏ b. job monotony.
   - ❏ c. computers.

9. You can conclude that a major employment concern of employers using mass production is
   - ❏ a. worker productivity.
   - ❏ b. the number of parts a product has.
   - ❏ c. the age of the equipment.

10. It is likely that as assembly line techniques are perfected, workers will
    - ❏ a. become less efficient.
    - ❏ b. take over jobs now performed by machines.
    - ❏ c. play a smaller role in mass production.

17　B　On the Assembly Line

We heard several weeks ago that Ford Motor Company was hiring ordinary workers, not just trained engineers. That was good news for me since I'm a good mechanic, but I have no special training. After I learned that I had a job, I looked forward to today because I would learn how to build a Model T.

When the other workers and I reported for work this morning, Mr. Henry Ford himself spoke to us. He said we would be making cars in a whole new way. He called it an "assembly line" production and said that every worker will have one specific job.

I'm now working on the line as a finisher. The car comes to me with its wheels, engine, and steering mechanism installed. As it rolls down the line, I grab a headlight, position it, and tighten the bolts that hold it in place. Across from me, my friend Jim puts in the other headlight. Behind us two other workers install the taillights. At first, the job seemed awkward, but after a few hours, I was sure I could do it with my eyes shut. Our team completed a car about every ten minutes, and I think we'll be able to complete one even faster with practice. Our work means that more cars will be available to people at a lower price. Because of us, someday soon everyone in America might have a car!

1. Recognizing Words in Context

Find the word *special* in the passage. One definition below is a *synonym* for that word; it means the same or almost the same. One definition is an *antonym;* it has the opposite or nearly opposite meaning. The other has a completely different meaning. Label the definitions S for *synonym*, A for *antonym,* and D for *different.*

_____ a. unusual

_____ b. general

_____ c. specific

2. Distinguishing Fact from Opinion

Two of the statements below present *facts,* which can be proved correct. The other statement is an *opinion,* which expresses someone's thoughts or beliefs. Label the statements F for *fact* and O for *opinion.*

_____ a. At first, the job seemed awkward.

_____ b. The narrator of this story installs headlights.

_____ c. Ford Model T's were built on an assembly line.

3. Keeping Events in Order

Two of the statements below describe events that happened at the same time. The other statement describes an event that happened before or after those events. Label them S for *same time*, B for *before*, and A for *after*.

_____ a. The headlights were installed.

_____ b. The taillights were installed.

_____ c. The engine was installed.

4. Making Correct Inferences

Two of the statements below are correct *inferences*, or reasonable guesses. They are based on information in the passage. The other statement is an incorrect, or faulty, inference. Label the statements C for *correct* inference and F for *faulty* inference.

_____ a. Ford pioneered the use of assembly lines.

_____ b. The workers found the work dull.

_____ c. The assembly line improved efficiency.

5. Understanding Main Ideas

One of the statements below expresses the main idea of the passage. One statement is too general, or too broad. The other explains only part of the passage; it is too narrow. Label the statements M for *main idea*, B for *too broad*, and N for *too narrow*.

_____ a. As each car rolls down the line, a finisher grabs a headlight, positions it, and tightens the bolt before the car moves on.

_____ b. Ford Motor Company hired unskilled workers to do specific jobs on the assembly line, greatly increasing the number of cars made.

_____ c. Division of labor, as on an assembly line, increases efficiency and productivity.

Correct Answers, Part A _____

Correct Answers, Part B _____

Total Correct Answers _____

80

The diversity of higher plant life in a rain forest is unrivaled by any other habitat in the world. The rain forests of the Amazon are believed to have tens of thousands of species of plants, many of them still unknown to scientists. Because rain forests have maintained relatively uniform warm, wet climates for long periods of time, many unique terrestrial species of plants and animals evolved there, and often these plants have medicinal properties not found anywhere else in the world. For example, quinine, used to fight malaria, and taxol, which has earned attention as a possible cancer treatment, were derived from plants indigenous to rain forests.

One feature of the natural, undisturbed rain forest is the layering effect created by the differing heights of trees and other vegetation. Below the tallest jungle trees, which are more than 150 feet (46 meters) high, are ones whose tops converge horizontally to form a dense upper canopy 60 to 100 feet (18 to 30 meters) above the ground.

Below the upper canopy, there is often an open space and then a second canopy created by smaller trees and other vegetation. Below this second canopy, the forest floor is dark, because most light is blocked out. So little sunlight penetrates to the ground in a heavily vegetated rain forest that the forest floor may have only a light cover of ground vegetation and extensive spacing between vines and tree trunks. Humans can sometimes travel through such natural forests with relative ease. It is only when the upper canopy is disturbed and sunlight penetrates to the forest floor that ground vegetation becomes so thick and dense that travel becomes difficult.

Dense jungles have numerous species of vines, which make unique adaptations to the minimal levels of sunlight on the forest floor. The large woody vine species are called lianas, which almost completely cover many of the trees in a rain forest. Some species of vines have evolved mechanisms to extract nutrients directly from the host tree. One example of the complex life cycles found among jungle plants is that of the strangler figs whose wind-borne seeds land atop tall trees. The strangler sends roots toward the ground and, as the vine grows, the host tree is eventually killed by a combination of factors such as a loss of light, competition for nutrients, and the actual physical pressure of the vine around the tree trunk.

Reading Time _____

Recalling Facts

1. Rain forest climates are usually
   - ❏ a. cold and wet.
   - ❏ b. warm and wet.
   - ❏ c. warm and dry.

2. Undisturbed rain forests are noted for
   - ❏ a. dense ground vegetation.
   - ❏ b. little vegetation.
   - ❏ c. the layering effect of the vegetation.

3. Large, woody vines are called
   - ❏ a. lianas.
   - ❏ b. canopies.
   - ❏ c. hosts.

4. A plant product used to fight malaria is
   - ❏ a. sap.
   - ❏ b. strangler fig.
   - ❏ c. quinine.

5. Taxol is a plant product that
   - ❏ a. may be useful in treating cancer.
   - ❏ b. is used to extract nutrients.
   - ❏ c. is used in gasoline.

Understanding Ideas

6. You can conclude from the article that jungle trees
   - ❏ a. are generally below average in size.
   - ❏ b. grow taller than other trees.
   - ❏ c. receive more sunlight than the vegetation below them.

7. A heavily vegetated rain forest is likely to have
   - ❏ a. light ground vegetation.
   - ❏ b. heavy ground vegetation.
   - ❏ c. many low-growing plants.

8. You can conclude that plant growth is related to
   - ❏ a. the amount of sunlight the plant receives.
   - ❏ b. the spacing between vines and tree trunks.
   - ❏ c. the plant's medicinal properties.

9. The article suggests that the unique plant life found in jungles is due to
   - ❏ a. lack of light.
   - ❏ b. unchanging weather.
   - ❏ c. competition for nutrients.

10. You can conclude that the properties of jungle plants are being studied by
    - ❏ a. medical scientists.
    - ❏ b. moviemakers.
    - ❏ c. space engineers.

Lost Miracles

Natives in the Amazon rain forests used curare from vines to make poison arrows. Today surgeons in modern hospitals use curare as a muscle relaxant during operations. Powerful medicines that help fight against leukemia and other forms of cancer have also come from jungle plants. Scientists are exploring rain forests worldwide in search of new "miracle" drugs.

In 1987 a botanist collected a sample from a tree in a Malaysian rain forest for the National Cancer Institute (NCI). NCI scientists began testing the sample to determine whether it had any special properties. Laboratory tests showed that an extract from the tree almost completely protected human cells from HIV, the virus that causes AIDS!

Scientists rushed to Malaysia to collect more tree samples. Unfortunately, however, where the source for the possible long-sought cure for the dreaded AIDS had grown, they found only dead stumps. The rain forest had been cleared for farming.

The tree stumps served as a reminder that valuable cures or treatments can literally vanish overnight. Each year an area of rain forest nearly the size of Massachusetts is destroyed. The continuing destruction of the world's rain forests has led to the extinction of thousands of species of plants and animals.

1. **Recognizing Words in Context**

   Find the word *properties* in the passage. One definition below is a *synonym* for that word; it means the same or almost the same. One definition is an *antonym;* it has the opposite or nearly opposite meaning. The other has a completely different meaning. Label the definitions S for *synonym,* A for *antonym,* and D for *different.*

   _____ a. qualities

   _____ b. nonattributes

   _____ c. possessions

2. **Distinguishing Fact from Opinion**

   Two of the statements below present *facts,* which can be proved correct. The other statement is an *opinion,* which expresses someone's thoughts or beliefs. Label the statements F for *fact* and O for *opinion.*

   _____ a. Scientists have discovered medicines from rain forest plants.

   _____ b. It is important to end the destruction of the world's rain forests.

   _____ c. Large areas of rain forest are destroyed each year.

3. Keeping Events in Order

Label the statements below 1, 2, and 3 to show the order in which the events happened.

_____ a. NCI scientists found that an extract from the tree protected human cells against HIV.

_____ b. The rain forest was cleared for farming.

_____ c. A botanist collected a sample from a tree in a Malaysian rain forest.

4. Making Correct Inferences

Two of the statements below are correct *inferences*, or reasonable guesses. They are based on information in the passage. The other statement is an incorrect, or faulty, inference. Label the statements C for *correct* inference and F for *faulty* inference.

_____ a. Scientists have developed valuable medicines from rain forest plants.

_____ b. The destruction of the Malaysian rain forest means that a cure for AIDS will never be found.

_____ c. The destruction of rain forests may prevent important medical discoveries.

5. Understanding Main Ideas

One of the statements below expresses the main idea of the passage. One statement is too general, or too broad. The other explains only part of the passage; it is too narrow. Label the statements M for *main idea*, B for *too broad*, and N for *too narrow*.

_____ a. The world's rain forests are a storehouse of plants that may provide new treatments and cures for deadly diseases.

_____ b. Scientists searching the world's rain forests for new medicines are being thwarted by rain forest destruction.

_____ c. An extract from a Malaysian tree was found to protect human cells from HIV.

Correct Answers, Part A _____

Correct Answers, Part B _____

Total Correct Answers _____

84

Most earthquakes take place on one of two great earthquake belts that girdle the world. These belts coincide with the more recently formed mountain ranges and with belts of volcanic activity. One of the earthquake belts circles the Pacific Ocean along the mountainous west coasts of North and South America and runs through the island areas of Asia. It is estimated that 80 percent of the energy released in earthquakes comes from this belt.

A second, less active belt is between Europe and North Africa in the Mediterranean region and includes portions of Asia. The energy released in earthquakes in this belt accounts for about 15 percent of the world's total. There are also connected belts of seismic activity, mainly along mid-ocean ridges including those in the Arctic Ocean, the Atlantic Ocean, and the western Indian Ocean and along the rift valleys of East Africa.

Most other parts of the world experience at least occasional shallow earthquakes that originate within 40 miles (65 kilometers) of the Earth's surface. The world's major earthquakes occur within well-defined, long, narrow zones between which lie large areas where few earthquakes occur. These long seismic zones correspond generally to the location of mid-ocean ridges and the so-called Pacific Ring of Fire.

The recently developed concept in modern geology of plate tectonics leaves little doubt that there is a direct relationship between the borders of the Earth's tectonic plates and the geographic distribution of earthquakes. According to the theory, the Earth's crust is broken up into a number of separate plates, and the edges of the plates rarely coincide with continental shorelines. Scientists have long known that these plate margins are extremely significant in earthquake studies, and major earthquakes located along these plate margins are associated with the geophysical processes of extrusion, subduction and overriding, and transcursion.

When a current of molten material from the upper mantle rises along the juncture of two adjoining plates, the plates spread apart, creating a rift valley filled with molten material. The rift valley is generally associated with the formation of volcanoes. This type of tectonic movement is known as extrusion. An excellent example of such a plate boundary is the one that forms the Mid-Atlantic Ridge. This ridge marks the zone where Africa was formerly joined to South America and where Europe split from North America some 200 million years ago. All mid-ocean ridges are sites of numerous earthquakes.

Reading Time _____

Recalling Facts

1. Most earthquakes take place
   - ❏ a. in the Indian Ocean.
   - ❏ b. in mid-ocean ridges.
   - ❏ c. on one of two great earthquake belts.

2. A theory states that the Earth's crust is broken up into a number of separate
   - ❏ a. oceans.
   - ❏ b. plates.
   - ❏ c. valleys.

3. Rift valleys are associated with the formation of
   - ❏ a. volcanoes.
   - ❏ b. earthquakes.
   - ❏ c. subduction.

4. There is a direct relationship between the geographical distribution of earthquakes and
   - ❏ a. the world's mountain ranges.
   - ❏ b. the borders of the world's tectonic plates.
   - ❏ c. temperatures around the world.

5. The Mid-Atlantic Ridge marks the zone where
   - ❏ a. Africa and South America were once joined.
   - ❏ b. South America and North America were once joined.
   - ❏ c. Africa and North America were once joined.

Understanding Ideas

6. The Pacific Ring of Fire is most likely named for
   - ❏ a. forest fires.
   - ❏ b. a group of volcanoes.
   - ❏ c. a series of earthquakes.

7. The article suggests that the study of earthquakes
   - ❏ a. has reached its peak.
   - ❏ b. is still unfolding.
   - ❏ c. is a guessing game.

8. Seismic activity is an indication of
   - ❏ a. mid-ocean regions.
   - ❏ b. tectonic plates.
   - ❏ c. potential earthquakes.

9. Where there is earthquake activity, there is also a likelihood of
   - ❏ a. tornadoes.
   - ❏ b. astrological destruction.
   - ❏ c. volcanic activity.

10. You can conclude from the article that scientists study earthquakes
    - ❏ a. to find out their effects.
    - ❏ b. to better predict when and where earthquakes will take place.
    - ❏ c. to further their understanding of pollution.

Mount Rainier is a majestic, snow-covered mountain rising above the city of Seattle, Washington. Underground, however, Rainier is not as peaceful as it looks. Like Mount Saint Helens to the south, which erupted in 1980, it is a volcano.

Inside Rainier, a geological drama is taking place. Superheated rock and gases from the center of the Earth are bubbling up. Their heat melts the ice on Rainier's peak, causing little rivers of water to run into the valley and mud slides that carry rocks. The gases inside the mountain also work on the mountain itself. Ever so slowly, they change rock into crumbly clay, and as the rock softens, it falls inward, creating holes that allow the gases to escape into the atmosphere. The process eventually weakens the whole mountain.

Scientists postulate that one day, a movement of the tectonic plates deep under the ground will allow lava, or melted rock, to rise up inside Rainier. Then the weakened rock may suddenly collapse, and lava, mud, and melted ice will pour out of Rainier down onto Seattle. As a result, elaborate warning systems and escape plans have been established. Rainier may not "blow" for 100 years. But scientists are quite sure that one day, the volcano will erupt. Will Seattle be ready?

1. **Recognizing Words in Context**

   Find the word *postulate* in the passage. One definition below is a *synonym* for that word; it means the same or almost the same. One definition is an *antonym*; it has the opposite or nearly opposite meaning. The other has a completely different meaning. Label the definitions S for *synonym*, A for *antonym*, and D for *different*.

   _____ a. offer a theory

   _____ b. do not believe

   _____ c. argue back and forth

2. **Distinguishing Fact from Opinion**

   Two of the statements below present *facts*, which can be proved correct. The other statement is an *opinion*, which expresses someone's thoughts or beliefs. Label the statements F for *fact* and O for *opinion*.

   _____ a. Mount Rainier is a volcano.

   _____ b. Mount Rainier is not as peaceful as it looks.

   _____ c. Internal heat melts the ice on Rainier's peak.

3. Keeping Events in Order

Label the statements below 1, 2, and 3 to show the order in which the events happened.

_____ a. The gases soften the rock.

_____ b. The rock crumbles, allowing the gases to escape.

_____ c. Hot gases bubble up inside the volcano.

4. Making Correct Inferences

Two of the statements below are correct *inferences*, or reasonable guesses. They are based on information in the passage. The other statement is an incorrect, or faulty, inference. Label the statements C for *correct* inference and F for *faulty* inference.

_____ a. Mount Rainier is unlikely to erupt again.

_____ b. A sleeping volcano is a potential danger to the people living nearby.

_____ c. Even a volcano that looks peaceful may be active inside.

5. Understanding Main Ideas

One of the statements below expresses the main idea of the passage. One statement is too general, or too broad. The other explains only part of the passage; it is too narrow. Label the statements M for *main idea*, B for *too broad*, and N for *too narrow*.

_____ a. Volcanoes are dangerous.

_____ b. Mount Rainier is an active volcano that may soon erupt.

_____ c. The superheated gases inside Mount Rainier melt its ice cap and cause mud slides.

Correct Answers, Part A _____

Correct Answers, Part B _____

Total Correct Answers _____

Fathers of Confederation

Canada owes its emergence as a nation to the vision and dedication of 36 Fathers of Confederation. In historic conferences, these dedicated leaders laid the foundation for establishing the Dominion of Canada.

Before 1867, British North America was a vast region of many fragments, with the most important fragment being Canada, which comprised Canada East (now Quebec) and Canada West (now Ontario). To the east were Newfoundland and the Maritime Provinces—New Brunswick, Nova Scotia, and Prince Edward Island. On the Pacific coast was British Columbia. The Hudson's Bay Company governed most of the interior.

Transportation between the various sections was extremely poor, and the vast interior would probably be lost unless it could be joined to a united Canada. The well-populated areas in most of the provinces were closer to the United States than to one another, and in 1849, there was a movement in Canada East to join the United States. Britain's free-trade policy, adopted in 1846, was seriously affecting the economy of the colonies, and many believed that the best way to safeguard trade and commerce was in union.

In Canada, the provincial government faced a crisis, chiefly because of hostility between the French-speaking Roman Catholics of Canada East and the English-speaking Protestants of Canada West. No political party could gain a working majority; so in an effort to break the stalemate, Liberal leader George Brown and his political foes Conservative leader John A. Macdonald and Georges-Etienne Cartier agreed to form a compromise government. The result was the Great Coalition of 1864. A major objective of the coalition government was to create a federal union of all the provinces.

The government scheduled the Quebec Conference, which opened on October 10, 1864, and was attended by delegates from every province. During the 17-day meeting, the 36 delegates and government officials approved 72 resolutions that became the basis of the British North America Act. They also scheduled a conference, which would meet in London.

The London Conference was held in December 1866 to complete the negotiations for confederation and to secure Britain's approval. Only six delegates from Canada and five each from Nova Scotia and New Brunswick were present. Prince Edward Island and Newfoundland had withdrawn from the talks. However, with virtually no parliamentary opposition, the British North America Act embodying the Quebec Resolutions was passed the following March, and on July 1, 1867, the Dominion of Canada was proclaimed.

Reading Time _____

Recalling Facts

1. In 1867, British North America became
   - ❏ a. the Canadian Confederation.
   - ❏ b. the Dominion of Canada.
   - ❏ c. Nova Scotia.

2. Before 1867, British North America was
   - ❏ a. a united country.
   - ❏ b. fragmented.
   - ❏ c. part of the United States.

3. In 1849, Canada East wanted to
   - ❏ a. become a separate country.
   - ❏ b. become part of the United States.
   - ❏ c. merge with Canada West.

4. The Great Coalition of 1864 was the result of
   - ❏ a. agreement among political foes.
   - ❏ b. a popular election.
   - ❏ c. pressure from Great Britain.

5. A key problem in British North America was
   - ❏ a. overpopulation.
   - ❏ b. transportation.
   - ❏ c. pollution.

Understanding Ideas

6. You can conclude from the article that the crisis in Canada resulted largely from
   - ❏ a. religious controversy.
   - ❏ b. transportation difficulties.
   - ❏ c. political conflict from within.

7. The article wants you to understand that controversy
   - ❏ a. can be settled by compromise.
   - ❏ b. usually leads to war.
   - ❏ c. results in the breakdown of government.

8. It is likely that when Canada became a nation, trade and commerce
   - ❏ a. diminished.
   - ❏ b. stayed the same.
   - ❏ c. improved.

9. You can conclude that when the Dominion of Canada was proclaimed, Great Britain
   - ❏ a. continued to handle Canadian internal affairs.
   - ❏ b. no longer handled Canadian internal affairs.
   - ❏ c. declared war.

10. The article suggests that Canada's emergence as a nation was the result of
    - ❏ a. pressure from the Canadian people.
    - ❏ b. the work of many people.
    - ❏ c. United States influence.

20 B   The Other Canada

The explorer Jacques Cartier claimed what is now Quebec Province for France in 1534, and its largest city, Montreal, was settled in 1642. In 1759 the British defeated the French and made Quebec a British province. Under British rule, the province prospered. Those who spoke only French were unable to speak the language of commerce, however, and they suffered as a result, becoming second-class citizens.

In the 1960s, the leaders of the French-speaking population began a drive for social change, and by 1968 a movement to separate Quebec from the rest of Canada had sprung up. In 1976 Parti Québecois, a separatist political group, came into power and passed laws that all provincial signs must be in French and all business must be conducted in French. The laws led many English-speaking firms to move to Toronto. A vote in 1980 on the question of whether Quebec should become a separate country was defeated when the majority voted to stay with the Dominion of Canada, but the matter was far from settled.

In 1991 an attempt to amend the Canadian Constitution to grant Quebec Province special status as a "distinct society" failed. Once again, the flames of separatism flared. So far, Quebec Province remains a part of Canada, distinguished by its strongly French character. But the question of separation also remains strong among its people and their leaders.

1. **Recognizing Words in Context**

    Find the word *commerce* in the passage. One definition below is a *synonym* for that word; it means the same or almost the same. One definition is an *antonym;* it has the opposite or nearly opposite meaning. The other has a completely different meaning. Label the definitions S for *synonym,* A for *antonym,* and D for *different.*

    _____ a. business

    _____ b. beginning

    _____ c. recreation

2. **Distinguishing Fact from Opinion**

    Two of the statements below present *facts,* which can be proved correct. The other statement is an *opinion,* which expresses someone's thoughts or beliefs. Label the statements F for *fact* and O for *opinion.*

    _____ a. Quebec prospered under British rule.

    _____ b. Montreal was settled in 1642.

    _____ c. Parti Québecois passed laws that all signs must be in French.

3. Keeping Events in Order

Label the statements below 1, 2, and 3 to show the order in which the events happened.

_____ a. Leaders of the French-speaking population began a movement for social change.

_____ b. An attempt was made to amend the Canadian Constitution.

_____ c. Parti Québecois was elected to power.

4. Making Correct Inferences

Two of the statements below are correct *inferences*, or reasonable guesses. They are based on information in the passage. The other statement is an incorrect, or faulty, inference. Label the statements C for *correct* inference and F for *faulty* inference.

_____ a. Unfairness toward those who spoke only French led to political revolt.

_____ b. The French have been more fair to those who spoke English than the British were to them.

_____ c. The culture of Quebec Province is different from other parts of Canada.

5. Understanding Main Ideas

One of the statements below expresses the main idea of the passage. One statement is too general, or too broad. The other explains only part of the passage; it is too narrow. Label the statements M for *main idea*, B for *too broad*, and N for *too narrow*.

_____ a. Canada's problems with Quebec Province are political.

_____ b. Social change in Canada led to the rise of Parti Québecois.

_____ c. The French history and culture of Quebec Province have led to political unrest in Canada.

Correct Answers, Part A _____

Correct Answers, Part B _____

Total Correct Answers _____

During the Renaissance, many families rose to princely power over Italian cities, mostly through the force of arms, intrigue, assassination, or subterfuge. The heads of these families made no attempt to disguise their absolute rule, but the Medici of Florence were a notable exception. The most eminent of all in their princely patronage of art and literature, the Medici rose chiefly by their intelligent use of wealth derived from commerce and banking. For a century, they maintained total authority in Florence behind the popular form of a republic.

Giovanni de' Medici (1360–1429) was the real founder of the wealth and power of the family, and his son Cosimo (1389–1464) conducted a vast banking and commercial business through branch houses in Rome, Venice, Geneva, London, and elsewhere. At the same time, Cosimo ruled Florence by skillfully making certain that his favorites were elected to the chief offices in the city. His position was not unlike that of an American political party boss, who maintains control over a city or state by using all sorts of underhanded tricks and favors without ever taking office. But Cosimo was a generous patron of art and literature, and his palace provided a refuge for scholars.

With Cosimo's grandson, Lorenzo the Magnificent (1449–92), the glory of the Medici reached its height. Lorenzo fortunately escaped the fate of his younger brother who was stabbed to death by Florentine enemies who plotted against the ruling family. Crowds seized the conspirators and tore them limb from limb.

Like his father, Piero de' Medici, Lorenzo continued the policy of untitled rule and patronizing the arts. Probably the most distinguished of the many talented people Lorenzo gathered around him was the youthful Michelangelo. Lorenzo was not only a patron of arts but also a man of learning and a poet whose verses were often scandalous. Excelling as one of the leading statesmen among the Italian princes, Lorenzo was a negligent business manager, however, and his family's bank closed shortly after his death.

Catherine de' Medici (1519–89), Lorenzo's great-granddaughter, became the wife of one French king and the mother of three others. She ambitiously worked to keep the power of the French monarchy undiminished for her sons.

After 1531, the later Medici abandoned the forms of a republic in Florence and assumed the title of duke of Florence. The Medici continued to rule under this title until 1737, when the family became extinct.

Reading Time _____

Recalling Facts

1. The Medici family were established in the city of
   - ❏ a. Rome.
   - ❏ b. Venice.
   - ❏ c. Florence.

2. The founder of the Medici wealth and power was
   - ❏ a. Lorenzo the Magnificent.
   - ❏ b. Cosimo de' Medici.
   - ❏ c. Giovanni de' Medici.

3. The Medici rule reached its height under the leadership of
   - ❏ a. Lorenzo.
   - ❏ b. Cosimo.
   - ❏ c. Giovanni.

4. The Medici fortune was derived from
   - ❏ a. government work.
   - ❏ b. scholarly pursuits.
   - ❏ c. banking and commerce.

5. The Medici rule ended when
   - ❏ a. the republic of Florence met its demise.
   - ❏ b. one Medici was stabbed to death.
   - ❏ c. the family became extinct.

Understanding Ideas

6. The Medici family could be characterized as
   - ❏ a. underhanded and conniving.
   - ❏ b. intelligent and sensitive to beauty.
   - ❏ c. democratic.

7. Compared to other ruling families of the Renaissance, the Medici were
   - ❏ a. distinguished.
   - ❏ b. weak.
   - ❏ c. tyrannical.

8. The basis of the Medici family's political control was
   - ❏ a. their patronage of the arts.
   - ❏ b. great wealth.
   - ❏ c. force of arms.

9. Enemies of the Medici were killed by crowds, which suggests that
   - ❏ a. the Medici were popular with the people of Florence.
   - ❏ b. the Florentine people resented the Medici.
   - ❏ c. Florence was a lawless city.

10. You can conclude from the article that rule in the form of a republic in Florence at the time of the Medici
    - ❏ a. was taken very seriously.
    - ❏ b. was a pretense.
    - ❏ c. represented the choice of the people.

Although he was one of the greatest artists of the Italian Renaissance and throughout history, Michelangelo had to overcome the protests of his father to practice his art. Michelangelo's father, a magistrate of the city of Florence, tried to beat his son out of what he considered his disgraceful desire to become a sculptor. It took the personal intervention of the city's ruler, Lorenzo de' Medici—known as Lorenzo the Magnificent—to persuade Michelangelo's father that there was a difference in status between an artisan who chiseled stones for buildings and an artist who chiseled statues.

Until the time of Michelangelo, artists had no status and received very little pay. The great accomplishments of Michelangelo helped change that. The sculptor of works such as David, the painter of the Sistine Chapel ceiling, the architect of Florence's Laurentian Library, Michelangelo raised artists from the status of laborers to an honored elite.

When Michelangelo died in 1574, his body was housed in a magnificent tomb that contained symbols of the three arts he had helped raise to high status: architecture, painting, and sculpture. The tomb is more than a monument to the great artist. It is a memorial to the victory of art itself.

1. **Recognizing Words in Context**

   Find the word *beat* in the passage. One definition below is a *synonym* for that word; it means the same or almost the same. One definition is an *antonym;* it has the opposite or nearly opposite meaning. The other has a completely different meaning. Label the definitions S for *synonym*, A for *antonym*, and D for *different*.

   _____ a. pound

   _____ b. win

   _____ c. soothe

2. **Distinguishing Fact from Opinion**

   Two of the statements below present *facts,* which can be proved correct. The other statement is an *opinion,* which expresses someone's thoughts or beliefs. Label the statements F for *fact* and O for *opinion.*

   _____ a. Lorenzo de' Medici stood up for Michelangelo against his father.

   _____ b. Michelangelo's father was a cruel person.

   _____ c. Michelangelo was a sculptor, a painter, and an architect.

3. Keeping Events in Order

Label the statements below 1, 2, and 3 to show the order in which the events happened.

_____ a. Michelangelo's father tried to stop him from becoming a sculptor.

_____ b. Michelangelo became a famous sculptor, painter, and architect.

_____ c. Lorenzo de' Medici supported Michelangelo's efforts to become a sculptor.

4. Making Correct Inferences

Two of the statements below are correct *inferences*, or reasonable guesses. They are based on information in the passage. The other statement is an incorrect, or faulty, inference. Label the statements C for *correct* inference and F for *faulty* inference.

_____ a. Without Michelangelo, artists would never have achieved any kind of status.

_____ b. Lorenzo de' Medici recognized Michelangelo's talent.

_____ c. Michelangelo's father felt that one's social status was more important than following one's dream.

5. Understanding Main Ideas

One of the statements below expresses the main idea of the passage. One statement is too general, or too broad. The other explains only part of the passage; it is too narrow. Label the statements M for *main idea*, B for *too broad*, and N for *too narrow*.

_____ a. Michelangelo, one of the great artists of the Renaissance, helped raise the status of the arts.

_____ b. The Italian Renaissance was a period in which the arts flourished.

_____ c. Michelangelo was the architect of Florence's Laurentian Library.

Correct Answers, Part A _____

Correct Answers, Part B _____

Total Correct Answers _____

The United States Endangered Species Act of 1973 defines an endangered species as any plant or animal that is in danger of extinction throughout all or a significant portion of its range. An extinct species is one in which living individuals of its kind no longer exist. The act identifies a threatened species as one to become endangered within the foreseeable future throughout all or a significant portion of its range. A rare species has no legal definition, but a rare species is any kind of plant or animal that occurs in low numbers in its natural range. About 1000 species in the world are now recognized as endangered or threatened with extinction.

Plants and animals have become extinct and new species have evolved since life began. Primitive human cultures may have eliminated some species, but the primary causes for species to become extinct have been natural ones. Major environmental changes resulted in the eventual disappearance of species unable to adapt to new conditions. Well-known natural extinctions include dinosaurs and other species represented in the fossil record.

Natural forces are still at work, but human activities cause most of the rapid and widespread environmental changes that affect plants and animals today. Many species have been unable to make the biological adjustments necessary for survival; thus, more species than ever before are threatened with extinction.

Destruction of forests, draining of wetlands, and pollution are environmental changes that may eliminate species in an area. Some herbicides and pesticides can have severe effects on certain species. Many species have small geographic ranges, so habitat alteration may eliminate them entirely. The logging of tropical forests, with their tremendous diversity of species with specialized requirements, has caused a steady increase in the extinction rate. Excessive hunting and trapping for commercial purposes also cause major problems. Plants also can be reduced to near extinction levels by extensive collecting. For example, many cactus species of the southwestern United States are now legally protected by state laws to prevent their removal.

The planned or accidental introduction of exotic species to a region can also lead to extinction. An introduced species often has no natural enemies to control its spread in a new environment, and native species may have no natural protection against it. The introduction of Dutch elm disease to North America, mongooses to Jamaica, and pigs to Hawaii resulted in the loss of native species having inadequate defenses.

Reading Time _____

Recalling Facts

1. An extinct species is one that
   - ❏ a. has few members.
   - ❏ b. no longer exists.
   - ❏ c. is endangered.

2. The primary cause for extinct species is
   - ❏ a. hunting.
   - ❏ b. the introduction of exotic species to a region.
   - ❏ c. environmental.

3. In addition to natural forces, a major threat to some plants is
   - ❏ a. insects.
   - ❏ b. extensive collecting.
   - ❏ c. overbreeding.

4. An example of an introduced species that has led to the loss of native species is
   - ❏ a. Dutch elm disease in Jamaica.
   - ❏ b. the mongoose in North America.
   - ❏ c. the pig in Hawaii.

5. A positive step toward saving plants and animals from extinction has been
   - ❏ a. declaring them legally protected.
   - ❏ b. labeling them extinct.
   - ❏ c. introducing new environmental changes.

Understanding Ideas

6. If current trends continue, plant and animal species will most likely
   - ❏ a. increase in number.
   - ❏ b. die out in greater numbers than in the past.
   - ❏ c. all be replaced by new species.

7. The article implies that the smaller the geographic range of a species,
   - ❏ a. the faster it is affected by changes in habitat.
   - ❏ b. the less likely it is to be affected by changes in habitat.
   - ❏ c. the more likely it is to change its habitat.

8. In order to survive environmental change in the past, animals have
   - ❏ a. changed their eating habits.
   - ❏ b. received government protection.
   - ❏ c. adjusted to new conditions.

9. Animals that migrate probably
   - ❏ a. have a lesser chance of surviving environmental changes.
   - ❏ b. cannot survive environmental changes.
   - ❏ c. have a better chance of surviving environmental changes.

10. You can conclude from the article that extinction of species
   - ❏ a. is a new problem.
   - ❏ b. has long been part of the natural order.
   - ❏ c. is becoming less of a problem.

Early American settlers encountered a remarkable sight—huge flights of passenger pigeons. Sleek, bluish gray, and about 16 inches (41 centimeters) long, the birds migrated from Nova Scotia down through Ohio and Kentucky to Arkansas and Texas. The naturalist John James Audubon estimated a single flock of passenger pigeons to contain more than a billion birds. They would pass by for hours, darkening the sky. A single breeding colony in Michigan covered 28 square miles (73 square kilometers). Their numbers seemed limitless.

By 1878, however, the flocks of passenger pigeons had begun to dwindle. No one knows exactly why, but there are several theories. The clearing of land by settlers reduced the birds' food supply and nesting grounds. Some birds died in storms and from disease.

Many birds were shot for food or for sport. Remarkably tame, they often roosted in the lower branches of trees, making it easy for hunters to pick them off.

The last known wild passenger pigeon was shot around 1904. By then, some passenger pigeons had been removed to zoos, but little was known at the time about captive breeding programs. The world's last passenger pigeon lingered in the Cincinnati Zoo until 1914, when it died of old age. An entire species had passed from existence.

1. Recognizing Words in Context

Find the word *single* in the passage. One definition below is a *synonym* for that word; it means the same or almost the same. One definition is an *antonym;* it has the opposite or nearly opposite meaning. The other has a completely different meaning. Label the definitions S for *synonym*, A for *antonym,* and D for *different.*

_____ a. multiple

_____ b. one

_____ c. unmarried

2. Distinguishing Fact from Opinion

Two of the statements below present *facts,* which can be proved correct. The other statement is an *opinion,* which expresses someone's thoughts or beliefs. Label the statements F for *fact* and O for *opinion.*

_____ a. Passenger pigeons were about 16 inches (41 centimeters) long.

_____ b. The last known wild bird was shot around 1904.

_____ c. Passenger pigeons' numbers seemed limitless, so there was no reason to protect them.

3. **Keeping Events in Order**

Label the statements below 1, 2, and 3 to show the order in which the events happened.

_____ a. The last passenger pigeon died in the Cincinnati Zoo in 1914.

_____ b. Settlement reduced the birds' food supply and nesting grounds.

_____ c. Audubon estimated the pigeons' numbers at more than a billion.

4. **Making Correct Inferences**

Two of the statements below are correct *inferences,* or reasonable guesses. They are based on information in the passage. The other statement is an incorrect, or faulty, inference. Label the statements C for *correct* inference and F for *faulty* inference.

_____ a. Contact with settlers contributed to passenger pigeons' extinction.

_____ b. Many factors may have contributed to the end of the passenger pigeon.

_____ c. People killed off the passenger pigeon by shooting the birds for sport.

5. **Understanding Main Ideas**

One of the statements below expresses the main idea of the passage. One statement is too general, or too broad. The other explains only part of the passage; it is too narrow. Label the statements M for *main idea,* B for *too broad,* and N for *too narrow.*

_____ a. Passenger pigeons are an example of the extinction of a species.

_____ b. The clearing of land by settlers reduced the birds' food supply and nesting grounds.

_____ c. The passenger pigeon, which once numbered in the billions, became extinct in 1914.

Correct Answers, Part A _____

Correct Answers, Part B _____

Total Correct Answers _____

Beginning in the 1780s during the time of the American Revolution, a movement to abolish the institution of slavery and the slave trade arose in Western Europe and the United States. Those who gave their support to this movement were called abolitionists.

From the sixteenth to the nineteenth century, about 15 million Africans were kidnapped and transported across the Atlantic Ocean to the Americas where they were sold as laborers on the sugar and cotton plantations of South and North America and the islands of the Caribbean Sea. In the late 1600s, Quaker and Mennonite Christians in the British colonies of North America were protesting slavery on religious grounds. Nevertheless, the institution of slavery continued to expand, especially in the southern colonies.

By the late 1700s, ideas on slavery were changing. An intellectual movement in Europe, the Enlightenment, had made strong arguments in favor of the rights of individuals. The leaders of the American Revolution had issued a Declaration of Independence in 1776, and in this document, they enunciated a belief in the equality of all human beings. In 1789 the French Revolution began, and its basic document was the Declaration of the Rights of Man and of the Citizen. There was a gradual but steady increase in opposition to keeping human beings as private property.

The first formal organization to emerge in the abolitionist movement was the Abolition Society, founded in 1787 in England. Its leaders were Thomas Clarkson and William Wilberforce. The society's first success came in 1807 when Great Britain abolished the slave trade with its colonies. When slavery showed no signs of disappearing, the Anti-Slavery Society was founded in Britain in 1823 under the leadership of Thomas Fowell Buxton, a member of Parliament. In 1833 Parliament finally passed a law abolishing slavery in all British colonies.

Slavery had been written into the United States Constitution in 1787, but a provision had also been made that permitted Congress to abolish the slave trade. Unfortunately, abolishment of the slave trade in 1808 coincided with a reinvigorated cotton economy in the South. From that time on, the North and South grew more and more different in economic and social attitudes.

Between 1800 and 1830, the antislavery movement in the North looked for ways to eliminate slavery from the United States. One proposal was to colonize Liberia, in Africa, as a refuge for former enslaved people. This experiment was a failure.

Reading Time _____

Recalling Facts

1. Abolitionists were
   - ❏ a. in favor of slavery.
   - ❏ b. against slavery.
   - ❏ c. unconcerned about slavery.

2. The European intellectual movement favoring the rights of man was called the
   - ❏ a. French Revolution.
   - ❏ b. Enlightenment.
   - ❏ c. abolitionist movement.

3. Thomas Clarkson and William Wilberforce were
   - ❏ a. members of Parliament.
   - ❏ b. writers of the United States Constitution.
   - ❏ c. leaders of the Abolition Society.

4. A failed experiment to eliminate slavery from the United States was to
   - ❏ a. colonize Liberia as a refuge for former enslaved people.
   - ❏ b. abolish the slave trade.
   - ❏ c. send former slaves to Europe.

5. The Declaration of Independence stated
   - ❏ a. belief in human equality.
   - ❏ b. an opposition to slavery.
   - ❏ c. a strong argument against the slave trade.

Understanding Ideas

6. Under the original United States Constitution, slavery was considered
   - ❏ a. illegal.
   - ❏ b. legal.
   - ❏ c. immoral.

7. The article suggests that slavery expanded despite protests because
   - ❏ a. economies depended on slave labor for profits.
   - ❏ b. religious groups did not take a strong stand.
   - ❏ c. antislavery laws were not enforced.

8. At the core of the disagreement over slavery between the North and South was
   - ❏ a. manufacturing.
   - ❏ b. religion.
   - ❏ c. the cotton industry.

9. You can conclude from the article that attitudes against slavery
   - ❏ a. resulted largely from movements within the United States.
   - ❏ b. grew out of antislavery movements around the world.
   - ❏ c. were found mostly in rural areas.

10. You can conclude that the effect of antislavery movements was
    - ❏ a. immediate.
    - ❏ b. slow to gather momentum.
    - ❏ c. to encourage increased slave trade.

23   B   Uncle Tom's Creator

Harriet Beecher Stowe was born in Connecticut in 1811. Her minister father often preached on the evils of slavery. The family later moved to Cincinnati, just across the Ohio River from the slave state of Kentucky. She could never forget the suffering of slaves that she saw firsthand.

In 1851 Stowe wrote and published *Uncle Tom's Cabin,* a novel about the days of the Fugitive Slave Law, when runaway slaves captured in the North had to be returned to the people who claimed to own them. The book became a best seller. Northerners were riveted by the story of the good old Uncle Tom, the saintly Little Eva, the impish Topsy, and the despicable plantation owner, Simon Legree.

Stowe's book awakened many in the North to the evils of slavery and intensified the growing rift between the North and the South. Stowe was a featured speaker at antislavery meetings throughout the North and welcomed by abolitionists in England.

The causes of the Civil War, which broke out in 1860, were extremely complex, but the feelings aroused by Stowe's book are often mentioned as a contributory factor. Abraham Lincoln, on meeting the author, is said to have commented, "So you are the little lady who wrote the book that started the big war."

1. Recognizing Words in Context

Find the word *despicable* in the passage. One definition below is a *synonym* for that word; it means the same or almost the same. One definition is an *antonym;* it has the opposite or nearly opposite meaning. The other has a completely different meaning. Label the definitions S for *synonym,* A for *antonym,* and D for *different.*

_____ a. lovable

_____ b. hateful

_____ c. amusing

2. Distinguishing Fact from Opinion

Two of the statements below present *facts,* which can be proved correct. The other statement is an *opinion,* which expresses someone's thoughts or beliefs. Label the statements F for *fact* and O for *opinion.*

_____ a. Harriet Beecher Stowe wrote a novel about Uncle Tom, Topsy, and Simon Legree.

_____ b. Stowe's novel deals with the time of the Fugitive Slave Law.

_____ c. The book intensified the rift between the North and the South.

3. Keeping Events in Order

Label the statements below 1, 2, and 3 to show the order in which the events happened.

_____ a. Abraham Lincoln commented to Stowe that her book had started the Civil War.

_____ b. Stowe saw the suffering of slaves firsthand.

_____ c. Stowe wrote *Uncle Tom's Cabin*.

4. Making Correct Inferences

Two of the statements below are correct *inferences,* or reasonable guesses. They are based on information in the passage. The other statement is an incorrect, or faulty, inference. Label the statements C for *correct* inference and F for *faulty* inference.

_____ a. Before Stowe wrote her novel, many northerners knew little about slavery.

_____ b. Stowe's novel was responsible for the Civil War.

_____ c. Stowe wrote from a belief that slavery was wrong.

5. Understanding Main Ideas

One of the statements below expresses the main idea of the passage. One statement is too general, or too broad. The other explains only part of the passage; it is too narrow. Label the statements M for *main idea,* B for *too broad,* and N for *too narrow.*

_____ a. Books can have an effect on people's thoughts.

_____ b. *Uncle Tom's Cabin* is a novel about the days of the Fugitive Slave Law.

_____ c. *Uncle Tom's Cabin,* by Harriet Beecher Stowe, helped educate people about slavery and possibly contributed to the start of the Civil War.

Correct Answers, Part A _____

Correct Answers, Part B _____

Total Correct Answers _____

Exercise and Fitness

The physical training of the human body to improve the way it functions is known as exercise. Exercise can be either active or passive. Exercise involving voluntary physical effort such as walking, swimming, bicycling, and jogging is known as active exercise, whereas passive exercise involves a machine or the action of another person. It includes many physical therapy techniques.

The body's capacity to perform work and defend itself against disease, infection, and the effects of physical stresses such as heat or cold is a measure of physical fitness. The degree of fitness required is related to the degree of stress the body must overcome.

Specific types of physical fitness are required for each person's body to meet special demands. Through exercise or work, muscles develop strength, and nerve-muscle coordination is improved. A body's ability to change posture suddenly requires orthostatic fitness. Orthostatic fitness can be determined by measuring how well the blood circulation can adjust to a quick change of posture, such as standing up after lying down.

Bursts of physical activity of maximum effort lasting less than 10 seconds require anaerobic fitness, which is the ability of cells to work without oxygen. Anaerobic activity involves sudden rigorous movements such as sprinting to catch a bus or the extra burst of speed needed to make a touchdown. Anaerobic exercise requires intense muscle activity that exceeds the capacity of the heart and lungs to supply oxygen to the cells. When anaerobic activity ends, the individual is left gasping for breath while heart and lungs work at supplying oxygen to reverse the oxygen debt condition. Any sport or activity that occasionally requires short bursts of energy followed by long pauses is considered an anaerobic activity.

Exhaustive efforts of longer duration require aerobic fitness, which involves a type of exercise that is distinguished by the body's ability to transport and consume oxygen efficiently. Running, swimming, bicycling, and cross-country skiing are examples of aerobic exercise. Aerobic exercise is characterized by the continuous, moderately strenuous effort that occurs at a pace enabling the heart and lungs to supply the oxygen needed by the muscles.

It is necessary to differentiate between health and fitness when describing the effects of exercise and physical conditioning. Health is thought by some to be the absence of disease. More specifically, it is the capacity of all body organs and systems to function at high levels. Fitness relates to performance and survival.

Reading Time _____

Recalling Facts

1. Exercise is classified as either
   - ❏ a. active or passive.
   - ❏ b. voluntary or involuntary.
   - ❏ c. physical or mechanical.

2. A measure of physical fitness is the body's capacity to
   - ❏ a. breathe rapidly.
   - ❏ b. work without oxygen.
   - ❏ c. perform work.

3. The degree of fitness required is related to
   - ❏ a. the effects of exercise.
   - ❏ b. a person's age.
   - ❏ c. the degree of stress the body must overcome.

4. Aerobic exercise is measured by
   - ❏ a. the body's ability to transport and consume oxygen efficiently.
   - ❏ b. how fast a person can run.
   - ❏ c. muscle strength.

5. Health is specifically defined as
   - ❏ a. the ability of body organs and systems to function at high levels.
   - ❏ b. the absence of disease.
   - ❏ c. physical conditioning.

Understanding Ideas

6. To be physically fit, a person should have the capacity to
   - ❏ a. run a mile in less than a minute.
   - ❏ b. exercise passively.
   - ❏ c. perform at an above-average level.

7. It is likely that a person who is physically fit
   - ❏ a. exercises every day.
   - ❏ b. gets sufficient exercise and proper nutrition.
   - ❏ c. is also a good athlete.

8. Compared to passive exercise, active exercise probably requires
   - ❏ a. greater physical effort.
   - ❏ b. less physical effort.
   - ❏ c. about the same physical effort.

9. Runners who compete in long races must be
   - ❏ a. orthostatically fit.
   - ❏ b. anaerobically fit.
   - ❏ c. aerobically fit.

10. It is likely that people who are not physically fit tend to
    - ❏ a. live longer than those who are.
    - ❏ b. die sooner than those who are.
    - ❏ c. live about the same length of time as those who are.

Toning Up

This will be a drag, Carrie thought, pulling on her workout clothes. Her sister had given her a trial membership in a health club, and she wasn't looking forward to the experience. The trainer positioned her in front of a mirror and pointed out her weak spots. "Your abdominal muscles need work," he said, "and you need to develop upper body strength. We can enhance your posture, too." He put her on a treadmill, and after a few minutes, he commented that her endurance could be a lot better, too. The trainer's assessment made Carrie feel miserable. I'm a physical wreck, she thought.

Carrie started going to the club and working out three times a week. At first, her arms, legs, and stomach muscles ached, but before long, she started to look forward to her time at the club. The trainer checked her progress. He started increasing the resistance on the exercise machines so that she was pushing and pulling more weight, and he increased the speed and the incline on the treadmill. Straining against the new settings, Carrie knew she was getting stronger. She felt proud of herself and was really enjoying the workouts. She could see by glancing in the mirror that in a short time, the effects of her workouts were beginning to show.

1. **Recognizing Words in Context**

   Find the word *enhance* in the passage. One definition below is a *synonym* for that word; it means the same or almost the same. One definition is an *antonym;* it has the opposite or nearly opposite meaning. The other has a completely different meaning. Label the definitions S for *synonym,* A for *antonym,* and D for *different.*

   _____ a. improve

   _____ b. enlarge

   _____ c. worsen

2. **Distinguishing Fact from Opinion**

   Two of the statements below present *facts,* which can be proved correct. The other statement is an *opinion,* which expresses someone's thoughts or beliefs. Label the statements F for *fact* and O for *opinion.*

   _____ a. Carrie had a right to feel proud of herself.

   _____ b. The trainer pointed out Carrie's physical weaknesses.

   _____ c. Carrie worked out three times a week.

3. Keeping Events in Order

Label the statements below 1, 2, and 3 to show the order in which the events happened.

_____ a. The trainer told Carrie that she needed to improve her posture, abdominal muscles, upper body strength, and endurance.

_____ b. The trainer increased the resistance on the machines.

_____ c. Carrie's sister gave her a health club membership.

4. Making Correct Inferences

Two of the statements below are correct *inferences*, or reasonable guesses. They are based on information in the passage. The other statement is an incorrect, or faulty, inference. Label the statements C for *correct* inference and F for *faulty* inference.

_____ a. The trainer was trying to push Carrie too quickly.

_____ b. Exercise improved Carrie's fitness.

_____ c. Carrie's self-esteem improved along with her fitness.

5. Understanding Main Ideas

One of the statements below expresses the main idea of the passage. One statement is too general, or too broad. The other explains only part of the passage; it is too narrow. Label the statements M for *main idea*, B for *too broad*, and N for *too narrow*.

_____ a. The trainer increased the resistance on the exercise machines.

_____ b. Carrie found that regular workouts at a health club greatly improved her fitness.

_____ c. Working out is good for you.

Correct Answers, Part A _____

Correct Answers, Part B _____

Total Correct Answers _____

An ambulance is an emergency vehicle that is used to transport people who are ill or injured. Usually an ambulance is used to carry an accident victim or a person with a serious illness to a hospital. Formerly used only for transportation, an ambulance today is often outfitted with sophisticated equipment and staffed by people trained in emergency medical service (Emergency Medical Technicians, or EMTs), who can begin care of the patient immediately.

In the United States, ambulances are required by law to carry specific equipment that is necessary for the care of patients. Kits for use in emergency care for breathing failure, heart disorders, broken bones, and burns are standard. The ground vehicles may be equipped with everything found in the critical and intensive care units of hospitals. Such items include equipment for intravenous procedures and for heart monitoring, oxygen and other gases, traction devices, and incubators for newborn infants.

Airplanes and helicopters, as well as ground vehicles, may be used as ambulances, and they are similarly equipped. Airplanes are used to reach settlements in remote areas such as the Australian Outback, where the Royal Flying Doctor Service has operated for many years. Helicopters are often used for emergency rescue work when other means of transport cannot reach the victims or transport them quickly enough. To be effective, an ambulance service must be able to respond to a call in less than 20 minutes. One ambulance for every 10,000 people is necessary for adequate emergency service.

Emergency treatment given immediately following an accident or a heart attack can save a life. A cadre of men and women has been trained to deliver treatments such as cardiopulmonary resuscitation, splinting of fractures, and control of bleeding. Basic EMT training is taught in about 80 to 150 hours, but advanced training in special areas, such as that for cardiac technicians, requires as much as 500 or more hours of training. Much of the training cost is paid for by the United States Public Health Service.

Probably the earliest formal use of an ambulance service was during the Crusades in the eleventh and twelfth centuries. Fighters wounded in battle were transported by horse-drawn carts back to their own lines for treatment. Out of this grew the Order of the Hospital of St. John of Jerusalem, or Hospitallers, which still operates worldwide in many areas of charitable medicine as the St. John's Ambulance Corps.

Reading Time _____

Recalling Facts

1. EMTs are people trained
   - ❏ a. to drive an ambulance.
   - ❏ b. in medical technology.
   - ❏ c. in emergency medical service.

2. To be effective, ambulances must be able to respond to a call in
   - ❏ a. less than 10 minutes.
   - ❏ b. less than 20 minutes.
   - ❏ c. 30 minutes.

3. Adequate emergency service requires one ambulance for every
   - ❏ a. 1,000 people.
   - ❏ b. 5,000 people.
   - ❏ c. 10,000 people.

4. Much of the cost of EMT training is paid for by
   - ❏ a. the American Medical Association.
   - ❏ b. trained technicians.
   - ❏ c. the United States Public Health Service.

5. Special EMT training is required for
   - ❏ a. setting broken bones.
   - ❏ b. cardiac care.
   - ❏ c. transporting victims.

Understanding Ideas

6. The advantage of modern ambulances over those used only for transport is that
   - ❏ a. patients can be treated before reaching the hospital.
   - ❏ b. patients reach the hospital more quickly.
   - ❏ c. hospital care is often unnecessary.

7. The article suggests that care provided on modern ambulances
   - ❏ a. increases the death rate.
   - ❏ b. reduces the death rate.
   - ❏ c. has no effect on the death rate.

8. The advantages of helicopters and planes over ground vehicles used as ambulances are speed and
   - ❏ a. the ability to reach remote areas.
   - ❏ b. reliability.
   - ❏ c. equipment capacity.

9. You can conclude from the article that the most critical aspect of life saving is
   - ❏ a. transportation.
   - ❏ b. emergency medical treatment.
   - ❏ c. cooperation from the victim.

10. You can conclude from the article that in the United States, emergency medical care is under the authority of
    - ❏ a. government.
    - ❏ b. private groups.
    - ❏ c. local agencies.

Ambulance Squads

In 1909 in Roanoke, Virginia, a boy named Julian Wise saw two canoeists drown because no one knew how to save them. He vowed then that someday he would become a lifesaver.

Wise never forgot his vow, and as a young adult, he organized ten volunteers into a first-aid squad. Three years later, the squad was able to resuscitate a sixteen-year-old boy who was near death by drowning. Newspapers picked up the story, and Wise and his crew began to get calls from other towns that wanted to establish first-aid squads.

The Roanoke squad grew from 10 to 58 members in the early 1950s, and the squad added equipment that enabled the members to deal with life-threatening situations. An article about them in the *Reader's Digest* created even more interest around the country and in Canada. By 1956 some 26,000 volunteers were staffing nearly 1,000 squads around the world.

Today's ambulance-squad members number more than 450,000. Many are trained in advanced life support. State-of-the-art equipment links them to doctors as they transport patients to emergency rooms and trauma centers and enables them to administer treatment. But they are still organized according to the principles of Julian Wise's first rescue squad, formed in 1928.

1. Recognizing Words in Context

Find the word *resuscitate* in the passage. One definition below is a *synonym* for that word; it means the same or almost the same. One definition is an *antonym;* it has the opposite or nearly opposite meaning. The other has a completely different meaning. Label the definitions S for *synonym*, A for *antonym*, and D for *different*.

_____ a. fail to restore

_____ b. revive

_____ c. comfort

2. Distinguishing Fact from Opinion

Two of the statements below present *facts*, which can be proved correct. The other statement is an *opinion*, which expresses someone's thoughts or beliefs. Label the statements F for *fact* and O for *opinion*.

_____ a. Roanoke's first-aid squad was organized in 1928.

_____ b. Today's ambulance-squad members number more than 450,000.

_____ c. The canoeists drowned because no one knew how to save them.

3. **Keeping Events in Order**

Label the statements below 1, 2, and 3 to show the order in which the events happened.

_____ a. Julian Wise saw people drown.

_____ b. Wise formed a rescue squad in Roanoke, Virginia.

_____ c. A magazine article about the rescue squad created nationwide interest.

4. **Making Correct Inferences**

Two of the statements below are correct *inferences*, or reasonable guesses. They are based on information in the passage. The other statement is an incorrect, or faulty, inference. Label the statements C for *correct* inference and F for *faulty* inference.

_____ a. Newspaper and magazine articles contributed to the spread of rescue squads.

_____ b. Rescue squads are less important than hospitals in saving lives.

_____ c. Towns quickly saw how rescue squads could be of help to them.

5. **Understanding Main Ideas**

One of the statements below expresses the main idea of the passage. One statement is too general, or too broad. The other explains only part of the passage; it is too narrow. Label the statements M for *main idea*, B for *too broad*, and N for *too narrow*.

_____ a. From ten volunteers organized by Julian Wise in 1928, rescue squads have grown to more than 450,000 members with state-of-the-art equipment.

_____ b. Rescue squads save lives.

_____ c. Today's ambulance-squad members are trained in advanced life support and linked to hospital emergency rooms.

Correct Answers, Part A _____

Correct Answers, Part B _____

Total Correct Answers _____

Answer Key

Reading Rate Graph

Comprehension Score Graph

Comprehension Skills Profile Graph

Answer Key

1A	1. a	2. b	3. c	4. b	5. a	6. c	7. b	8. c	9. b	10. c
1B	1. A, D, S	2. F, O, F	3. 3, 2, 1		4. F, C, C		5. B, N, M			
2A	1. c	2. b	3. c	4. b	5. b	6. a	7. b	8. b	9. b	10. c
2B	1. S, D, A	2. O, F, F	3. 2, 1, 3		4. F, C, C		5. N, B, M			
3A	1. b	2. a	3. b	4. c	5. c	6. a	7. a	8. b	9. a	10. b
3B	1. D, A, S	2. F, O, F	3. 1, 3, 2		4. C, C, F		5. B, M, N			
4A	1. b	2. c	3. a	4. b	5. a	6. a	7. b	8. b	9. a	10. c
4B	1. S, D, A	2. O, F, F	3. 2, 3, 1		4. C, F, C		5. N, B, M			
5A	1. c	2. b	3. b	4. a	5. c	6. a	7. b	8. c	9. c	10. a
5B	1. A, S, D	2. O, F, F	3. 1, 2, 3		4. C, F, C		5. M, N, B			
6A	1. b	2. c	3. b	4. c	5. b	6. b	7. c	8. a	9. b	10. c
6B	1. D, S, A	2. F, F, O	3. 3, 1, 2		4. C, C, F		5. N, M, B			
7A	1. a	2. b	3. b	4. c	5. a	6. c	7. a	8. a	9. c	10. c
7B	1. S, A, D	2. F, F, O	3. 2, 1, 3		4. F, C, C		5. N, M, B			
8A	1. c	2. c	3. b	4. a	5. b	6. c	7. a	8. c	9. b	10. a
8B	1. A, S, D	2. O, F, F	3. 1, 3, 2		4. F, C, C		5. B, N, M			
9A	1. b	2. b	3. a	4. a	5. b	6. a	7. b	8. b	9. b	10. c
9B	1. A, D, S	2. F, O, F	3. 2, 1, 3		4. C, F, C		5. B, N, M			
10A	1. c	2. b	3. c	4. a	5. c	6. b	7. c	8. b	9. c	10. c
10B	1. D, S, A	2. O, F, F	3. S, B, S		4. F, C, C		5. N, B, M			
11A	1. c	2. a	3. b	4. b	5. c	6. b	7. b	8. a	9. a	10. b
11B	1. D, A, S	2. O, F, F	3. S, A, S		4. F, C, C		5. M, B, N			
12A	1. a	2. a	3. c	4. a	5. c	6. b	7. a	8. b	9. c	10. c
12B	1. A, D, S	2. F, F, O	3. 3, 1, 2		4. C, F, C		5. M, N, B			
13A	1. b	2. c	3. c	4. b	5. a	6. a	7. b	8. b	9. c	10. b
13B	1. D, S, A	2. F, O, F	3. 3, 1, 2		4. F, C, C		5. M, B, N			

14A	1. b	2. a	3. b	4. c	5. c	6. b	7. c	8. a	9. c	10. a
14B	1. D, A, S	2. F, F, O	3. 1, 3, 2	4. C, F, C	5. B, N, M					
15A	1. b	2. c	3. b	4. b	5. b	6. c	7. c	8. a	9. b	10. c
15B	1. D, S, A	2. O, F, F	3. 2, 3, 1	4. C, C, F	5. N, M, B					
16A	1. c	2. a	3. a	4. b	5. a	6. c	7. b	8. c	9. b	10. a
16B	1. S, A, D	2. F, F, O	3. B, S, S	4. C, C, F	5. N, M, B					
17A	1. a	2. a	3. b	4. c	5. c	6. c	7. a	8. b	9. a	10. c
17B	1. D, A, S	2. O, F, F	3. S, S, B	4. C, F, C	5. N, M, B					
18A	1. b	2. c	3. a	4. c	5. a	6. c	7. a	8. a	9. b	10. a
18B	1. S, A, D	2. F, O, F	3. 2, 3, 1	4. C, F, C	5. B, M, N					
19A	1. c	2. b	3. a	4. b	5. a	6. b	7. b	8. c	9. c	10. b
19B	1. S, A, D	2. F, O, F	3. 2, 3, 1	4. F, C, C	5. B, M, N					
20A	1. b	2. b	3. b	4. a	5. b	6. c	7. a	8. c	9. b	10. b
20B	1. S, D, A	2. O, F, F	3. 1, 3, 2	4. C, F, C	5. B, N, M					
21A	1. c	2. c	3. a	4. c	5. c	6. b	7. a	8. b	9. a	10. b
21B	1. S, D, A	2. F, O, F	3. 1, 3, 2	4. F, C, C	5. M, B, N					
22A	1. b	2. c	3. b	4. c	5. a	6. b	7. a	8. c	9. c	10. b
22B	1. A, S, D	2. F, F, O	3. 3, 2, 1	4. C, C, F	5. B, N, M					
23A	1. b	2. b	3. c	4. a	5. a	6. b	7. a	8. c	9. b	10. b
23B	1. A, S, D	2. F, F, O	3. 3, 1, 2	4. C, F, C	5. B, N, M					
24A	1. a	2. c	3. c	4. a	5. a	6. c	7. b	8. a	9. c	10. b
24B	1. S, D, A	2. O, F, F	3. 2, 3, 1	4. F, C, C	5. N, M, B					
25A	1. c	2. b	3. c	4. c	5. b	6. a	7. b	8. a	9. b	10. a
25B	1. A, S, D	2. F, F, O	3. 1, 2, 3	4. C, F, C	5. M, B, N					

READING RATE

Put an X on the line above each lesson number to show your reading time and words-per-minute rate for that unit.

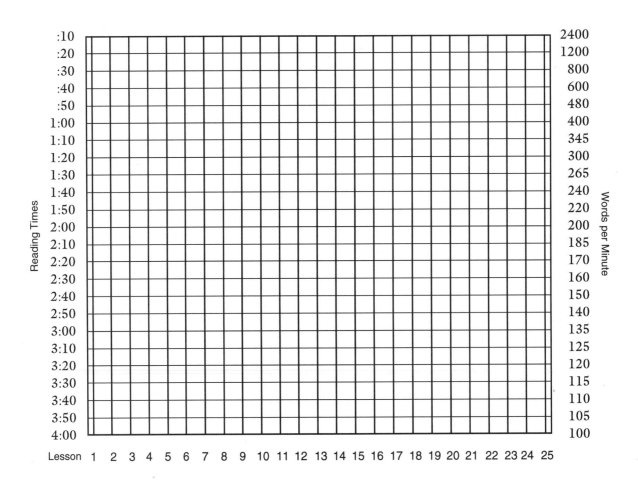

COMPREHENSION SCORE

Put an X on the line above each lesson number to indicate your total correct answers and comprehension score for that unit.

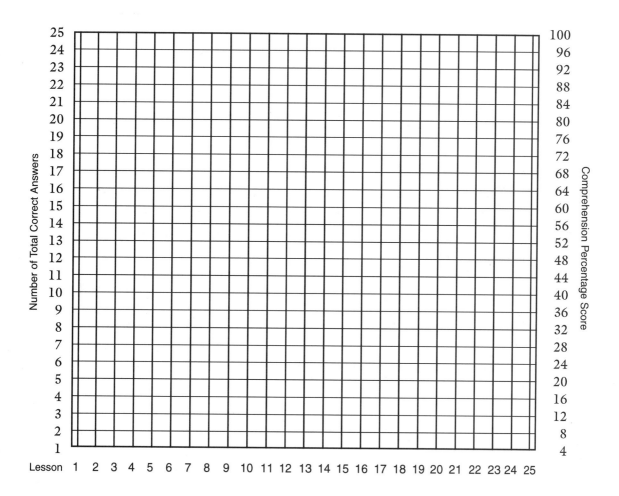

COMPREHENSION SKILLS PROFILE

Put an X in the box above each question type to indicate an incorrect reponse to any part of that question.

Lesson	Recognizing Words in Context	Distinguishing Fact from Opinion	Keeping Events in Order	Making Correct Inferences	Understanding Main Ideas
1					
2					
3					
4					
5					
6					
7					
8					
9					
10					
11					
12					
13					
14					
15					
16					
17					
18					
19					
20					
21					
22					
23					
24					
25					